THE
BIG BOOK
of
PATTERNS

ADULT COLORING BOOK

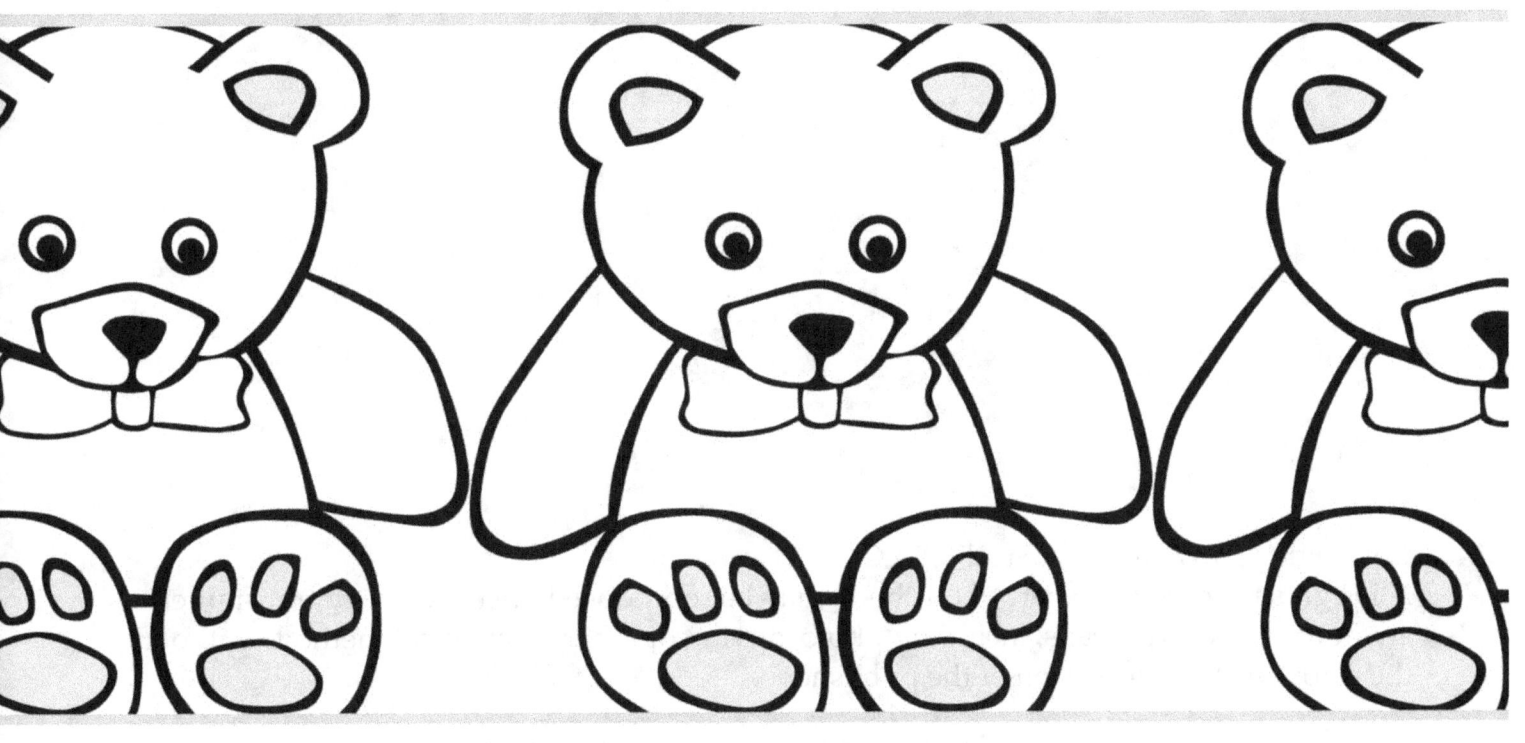

VOLUME 2

by DAN GREENE

DEDICATION

To You!

Acknowledgements

Some of the images in this book were modified under Creative Commons License 3.0. A link to the license is provided here: creativecommons.org/license

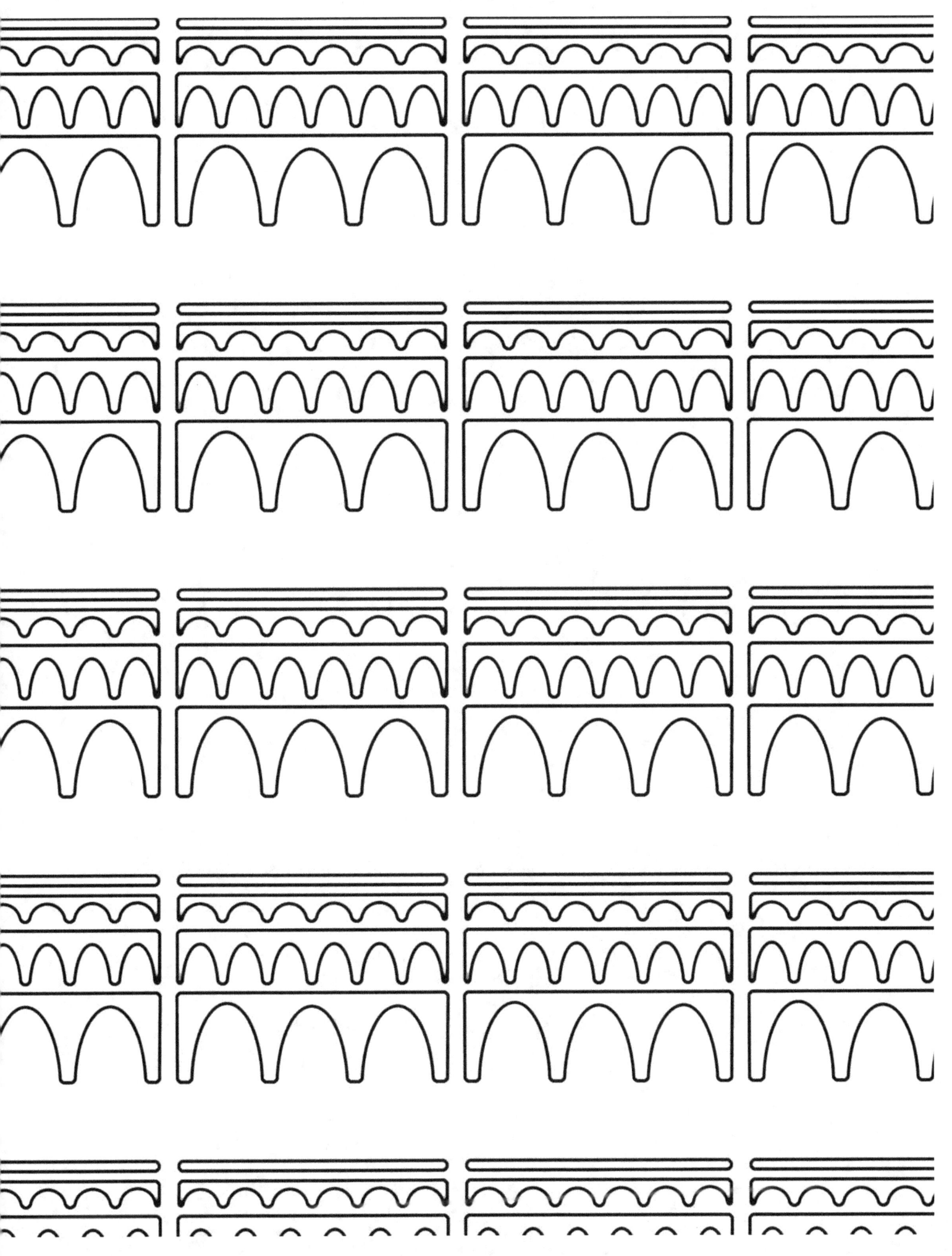

Doodles

Doodles

Doodles

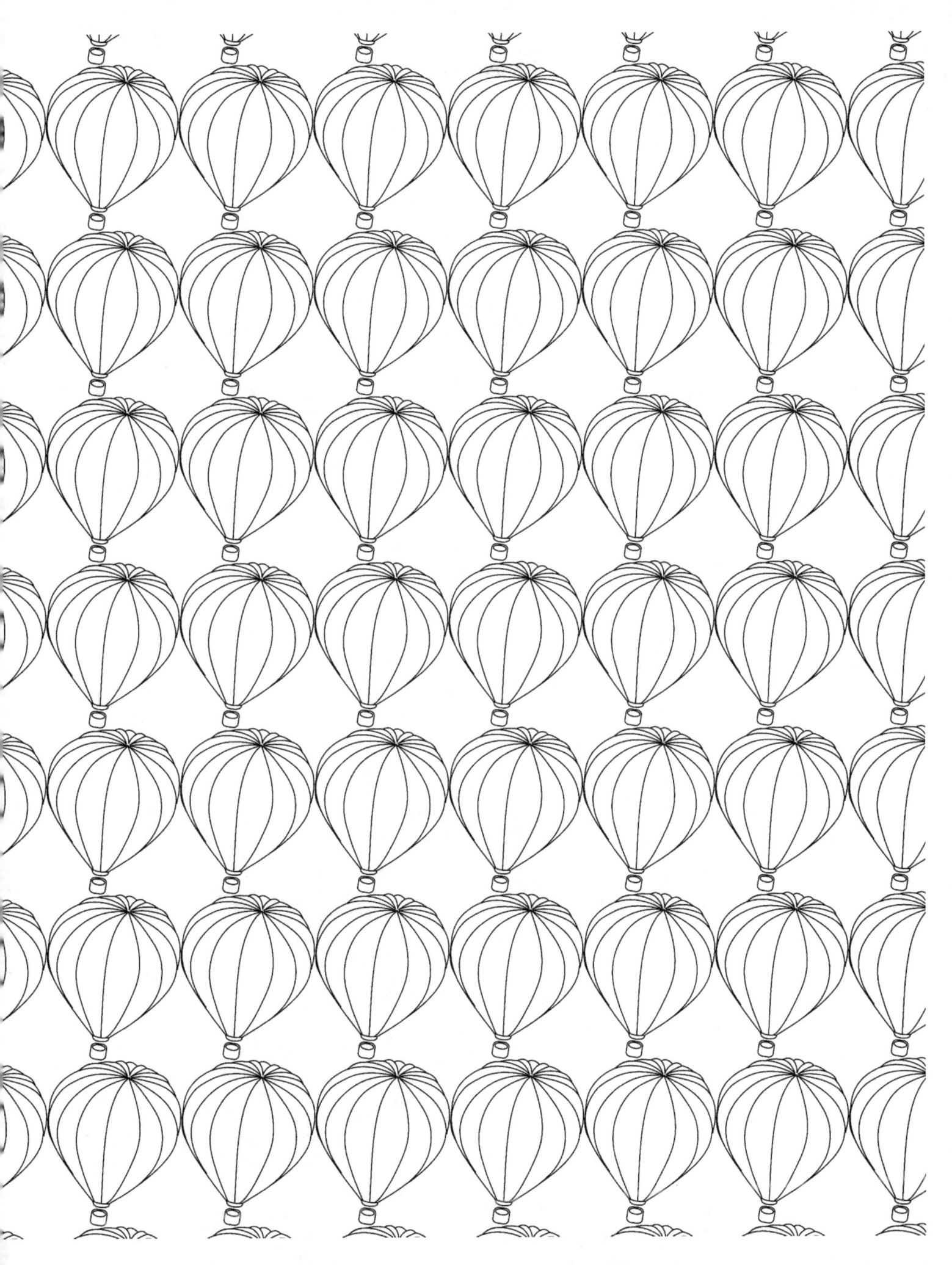

Doodles

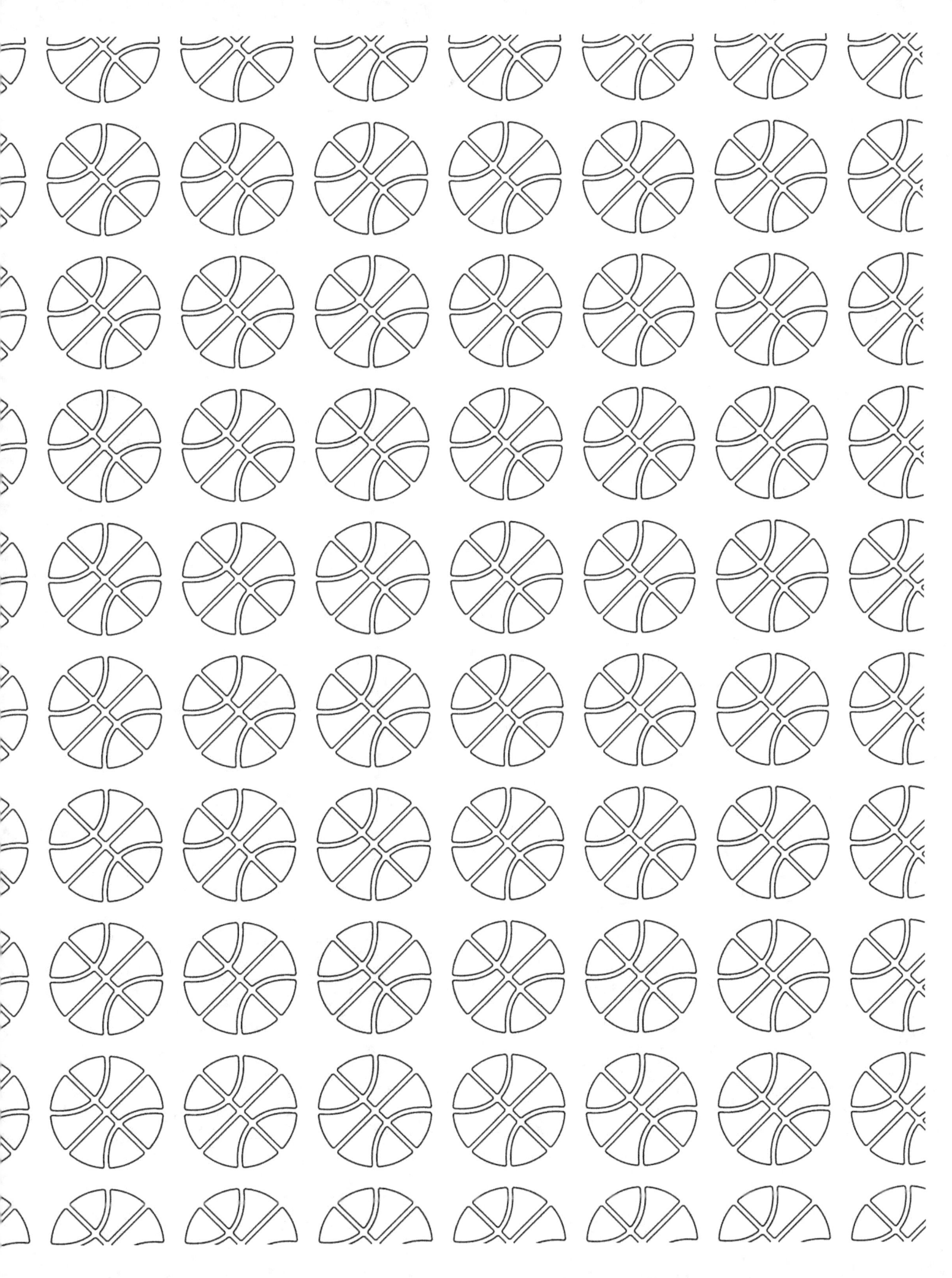

Doodles

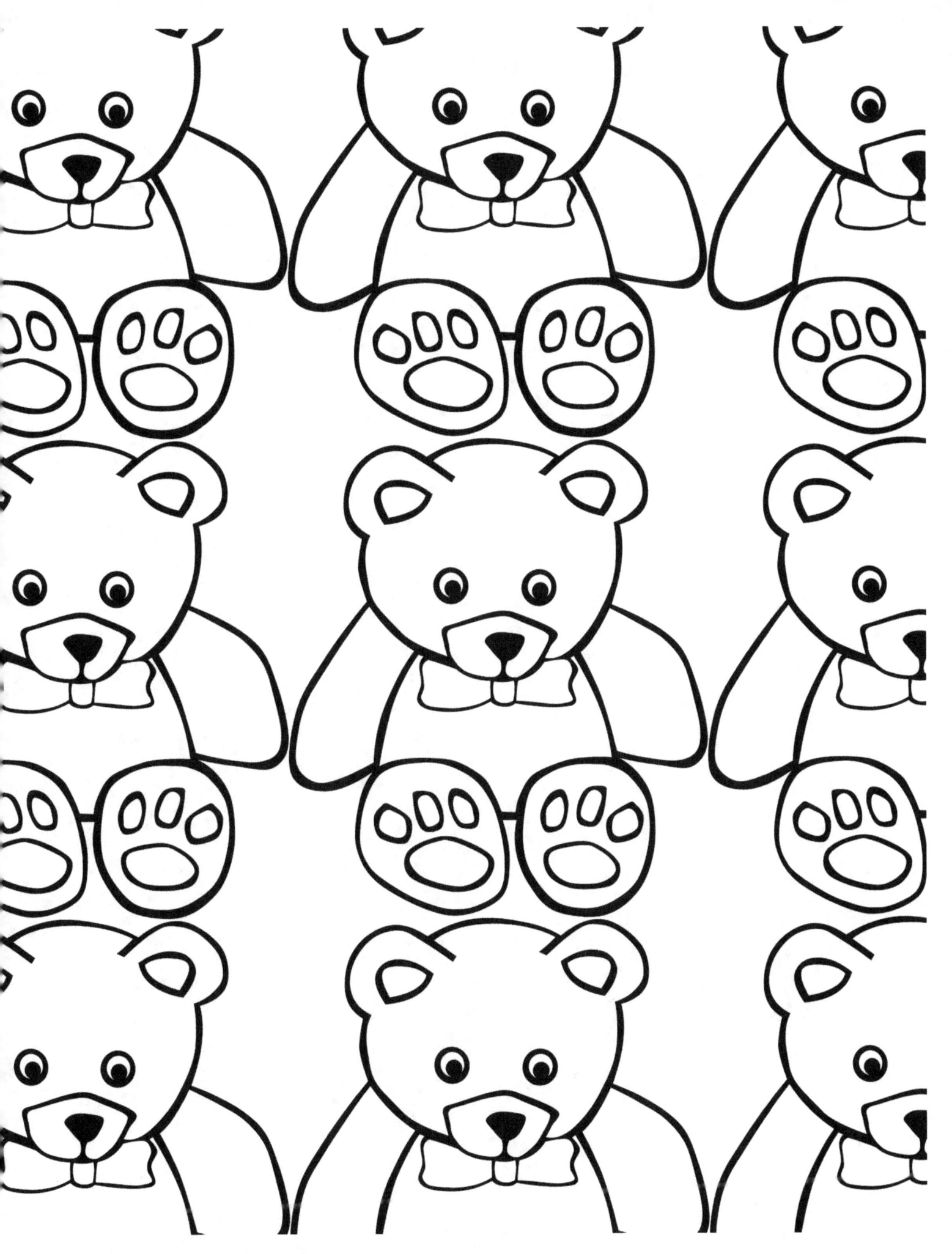

Doodles

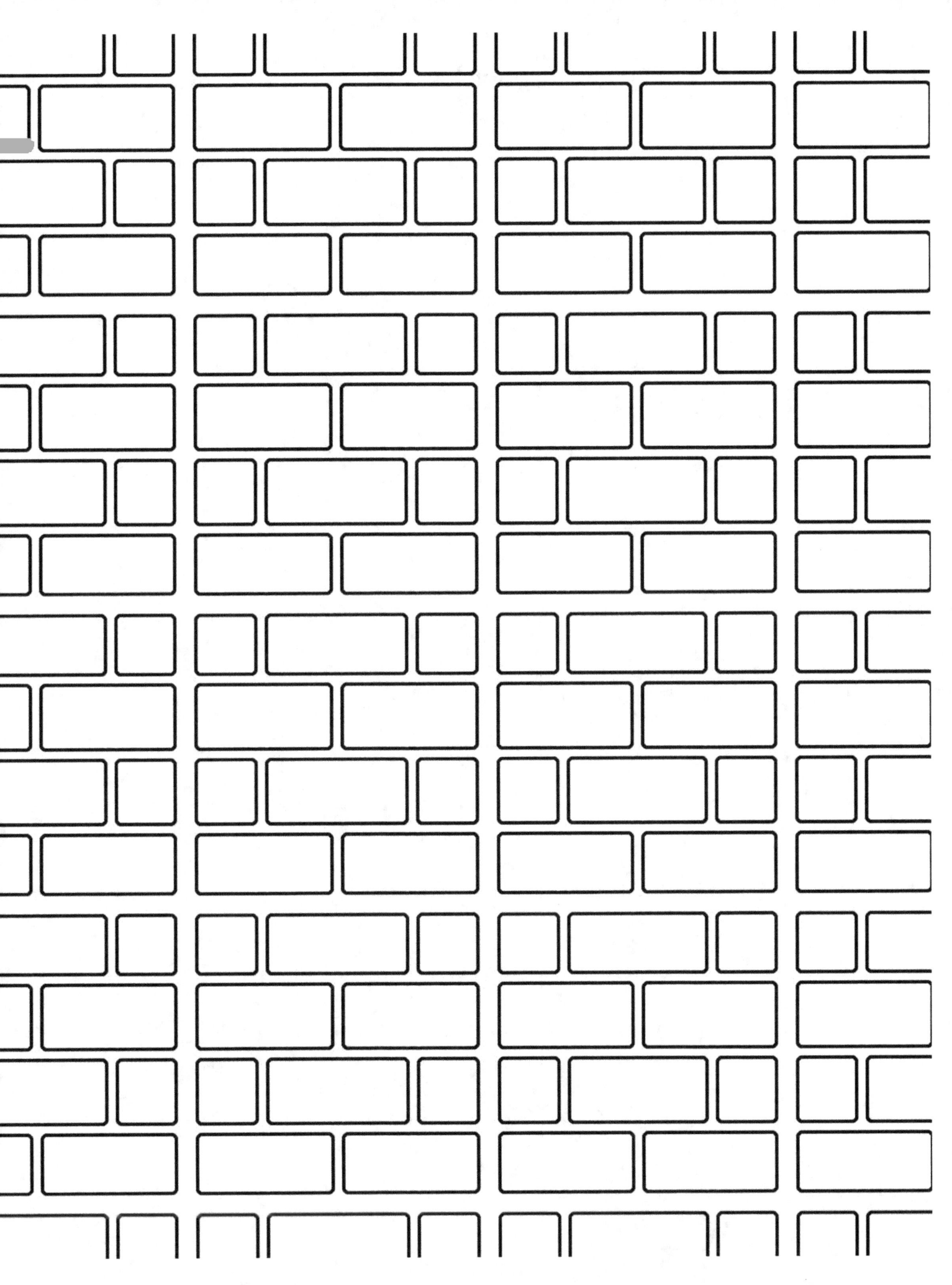

Doodles

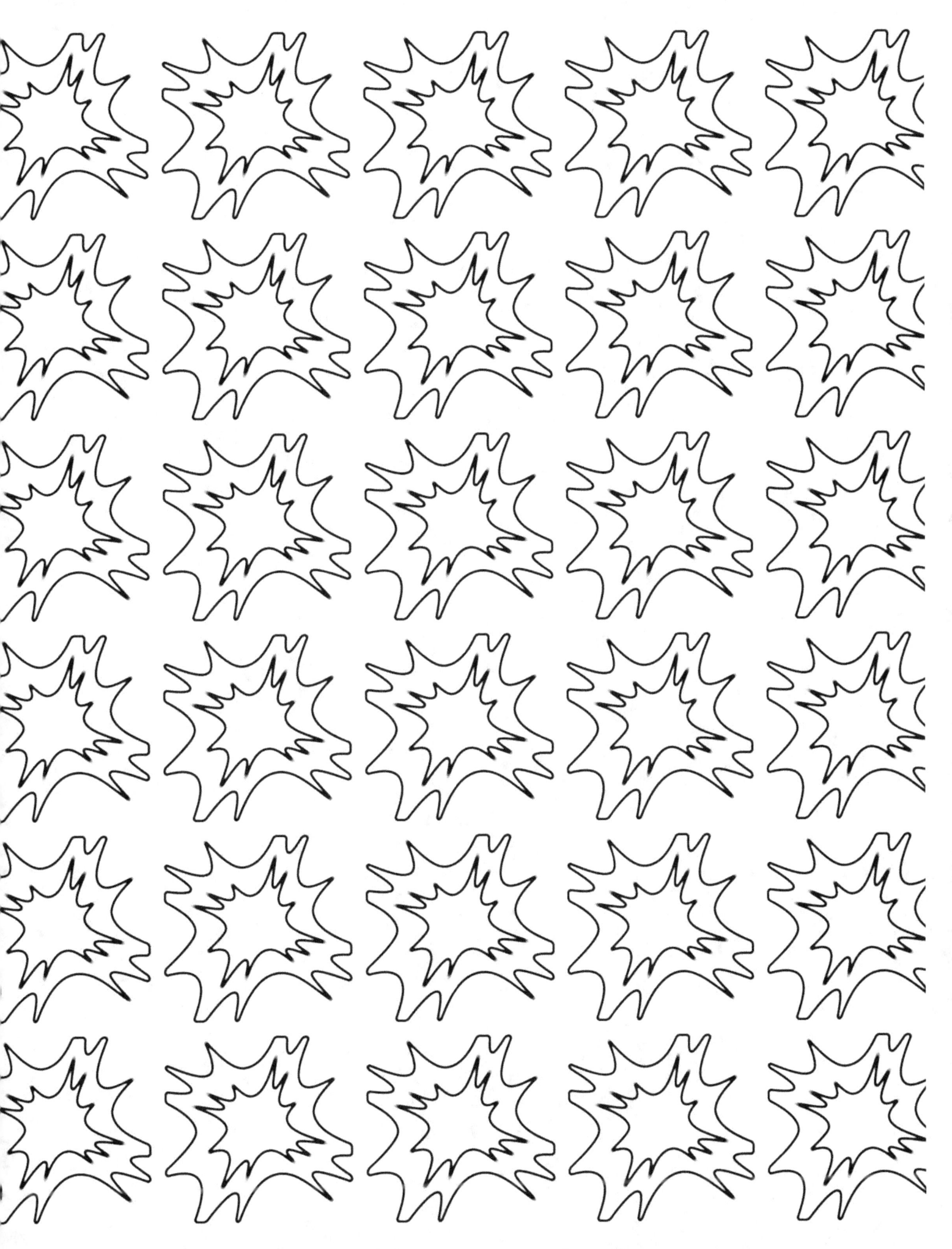

Doodles

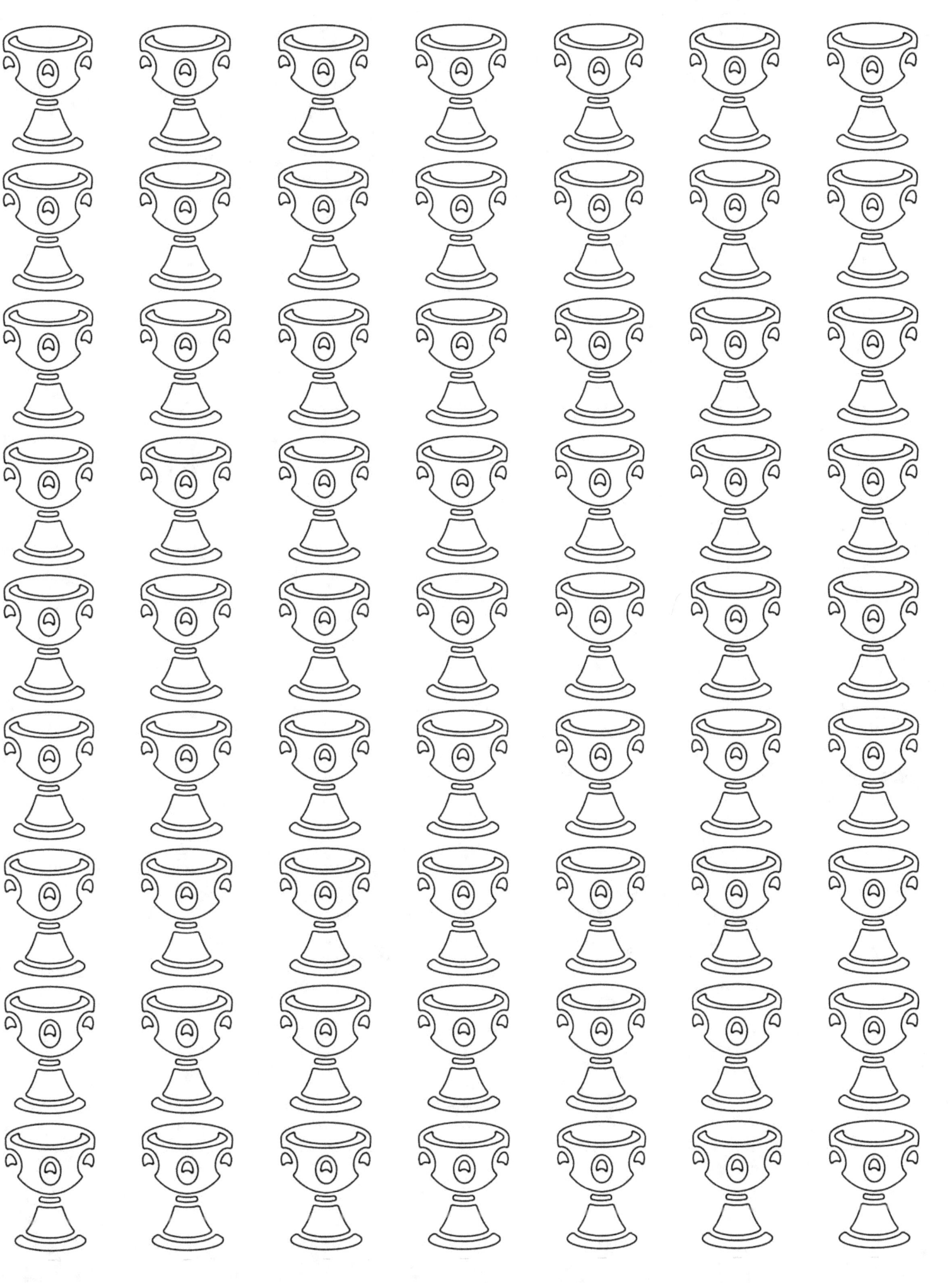

Doodles

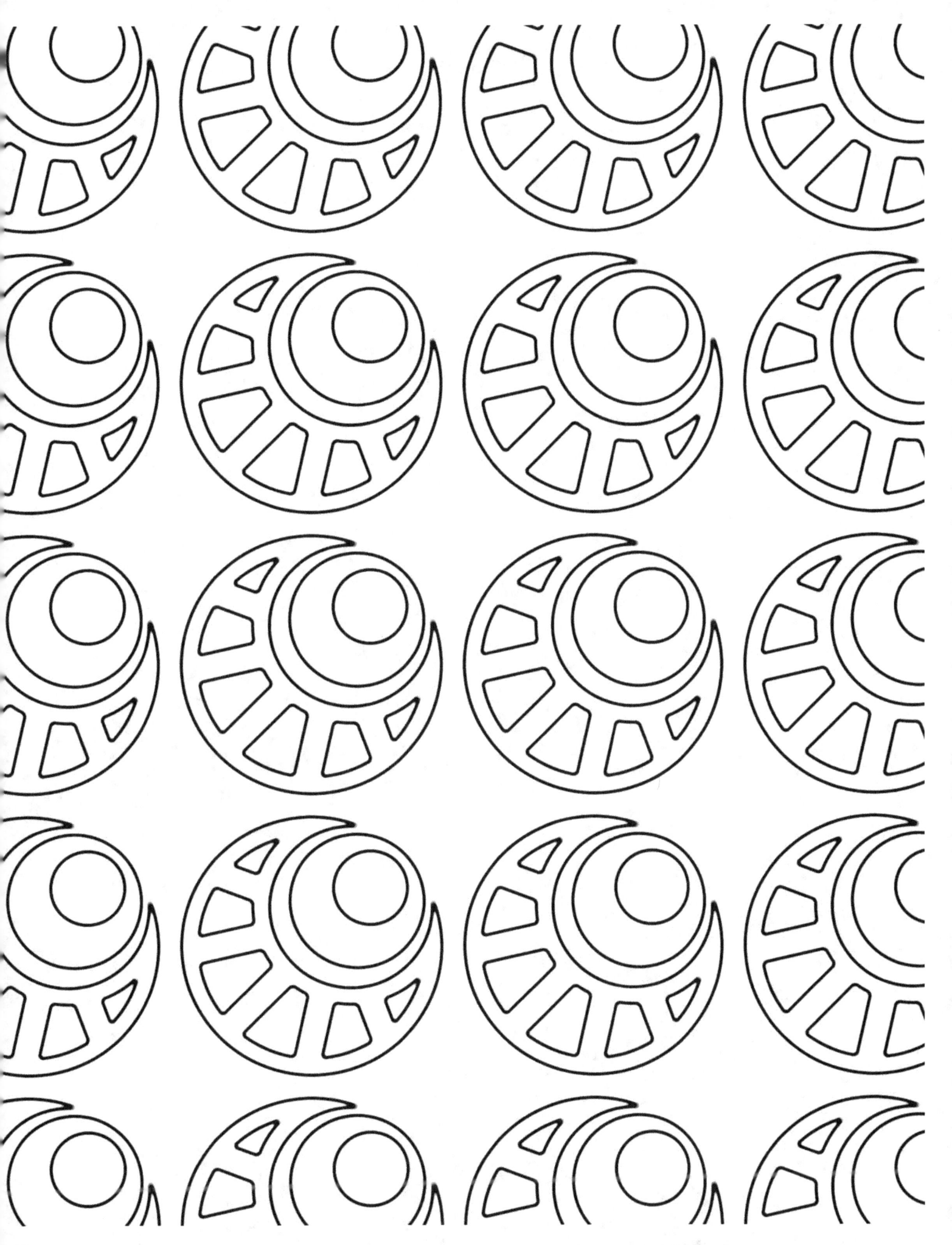

Doodles

Doodles

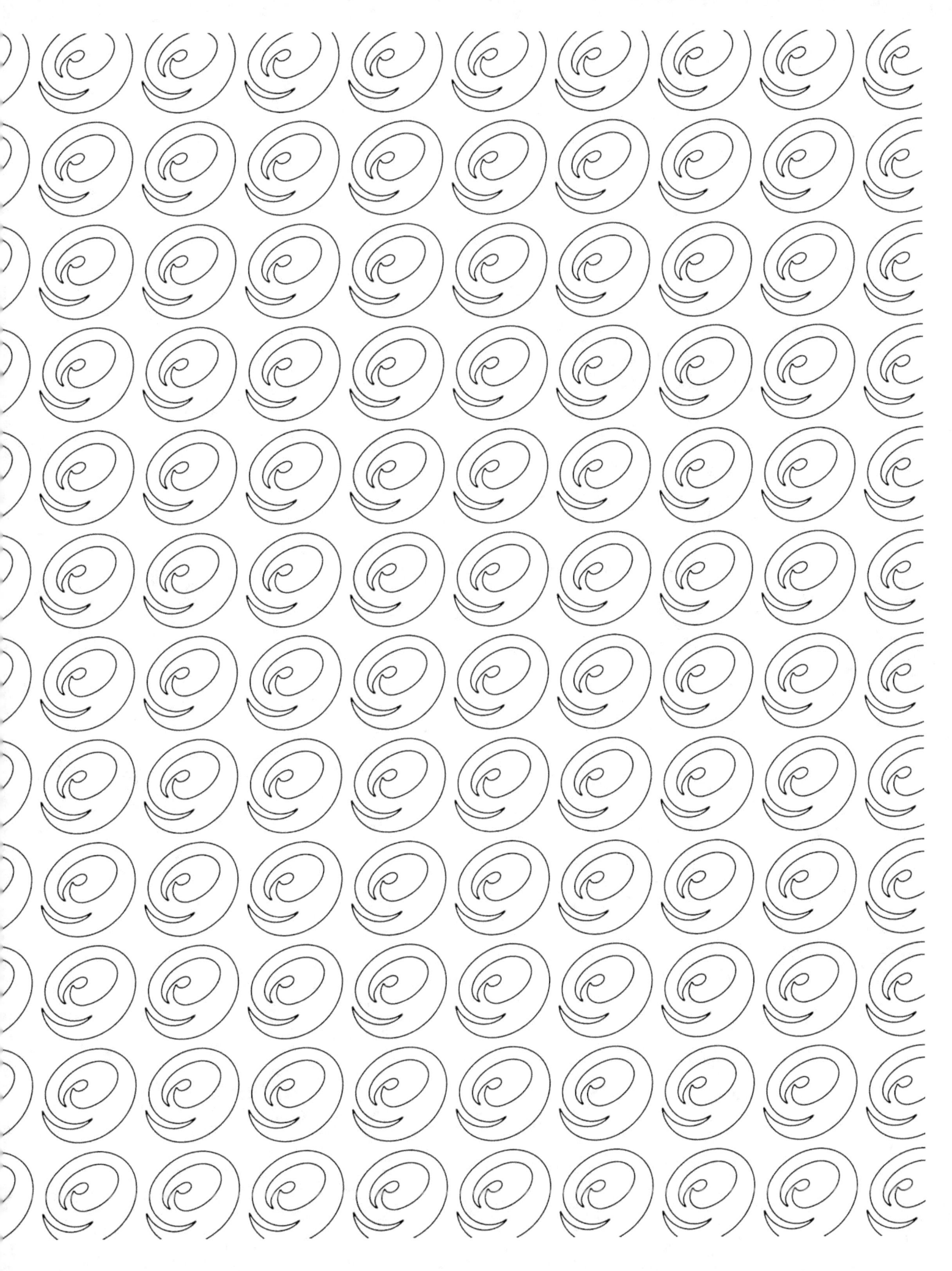

Doodles

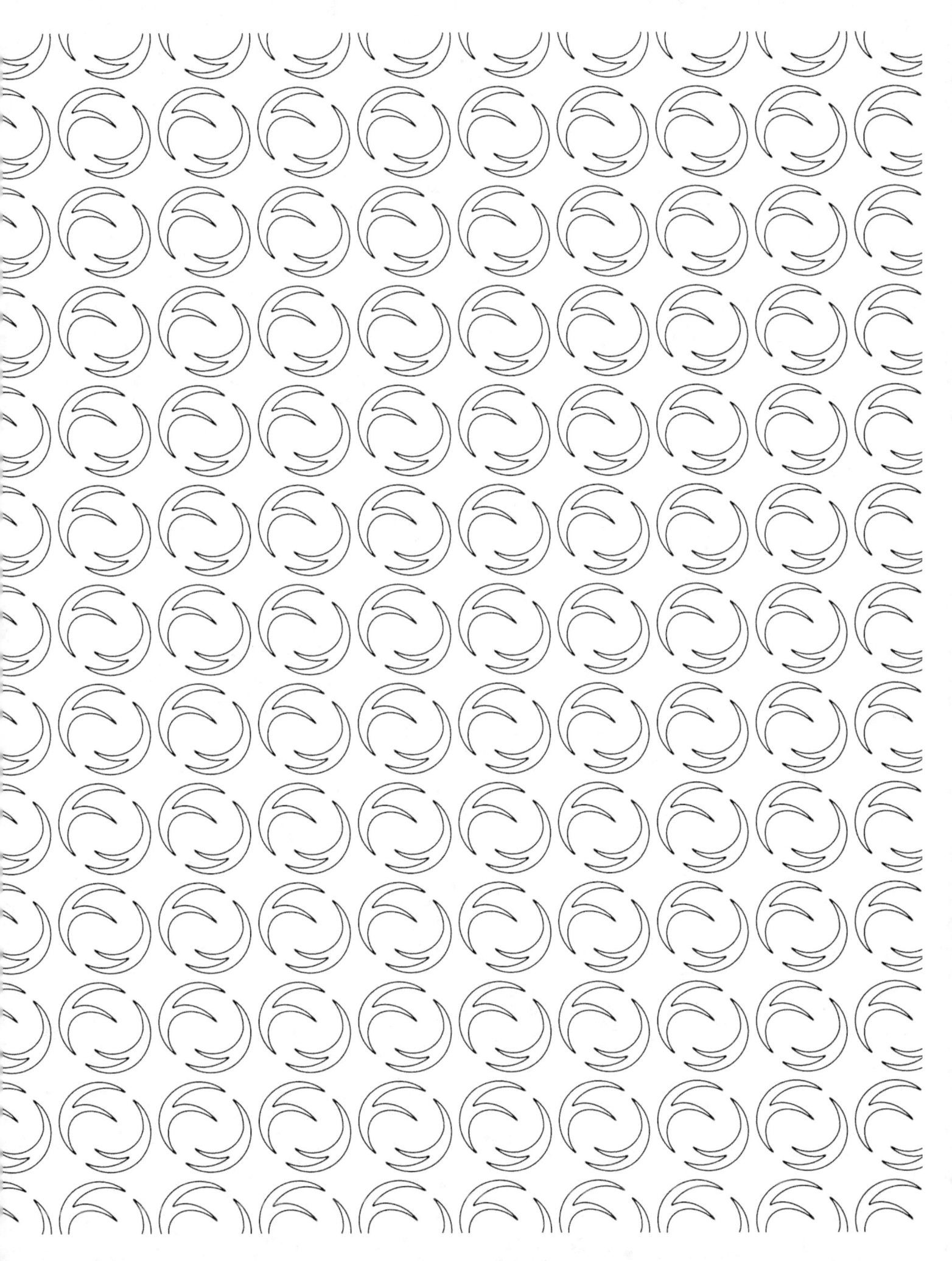

Doodles

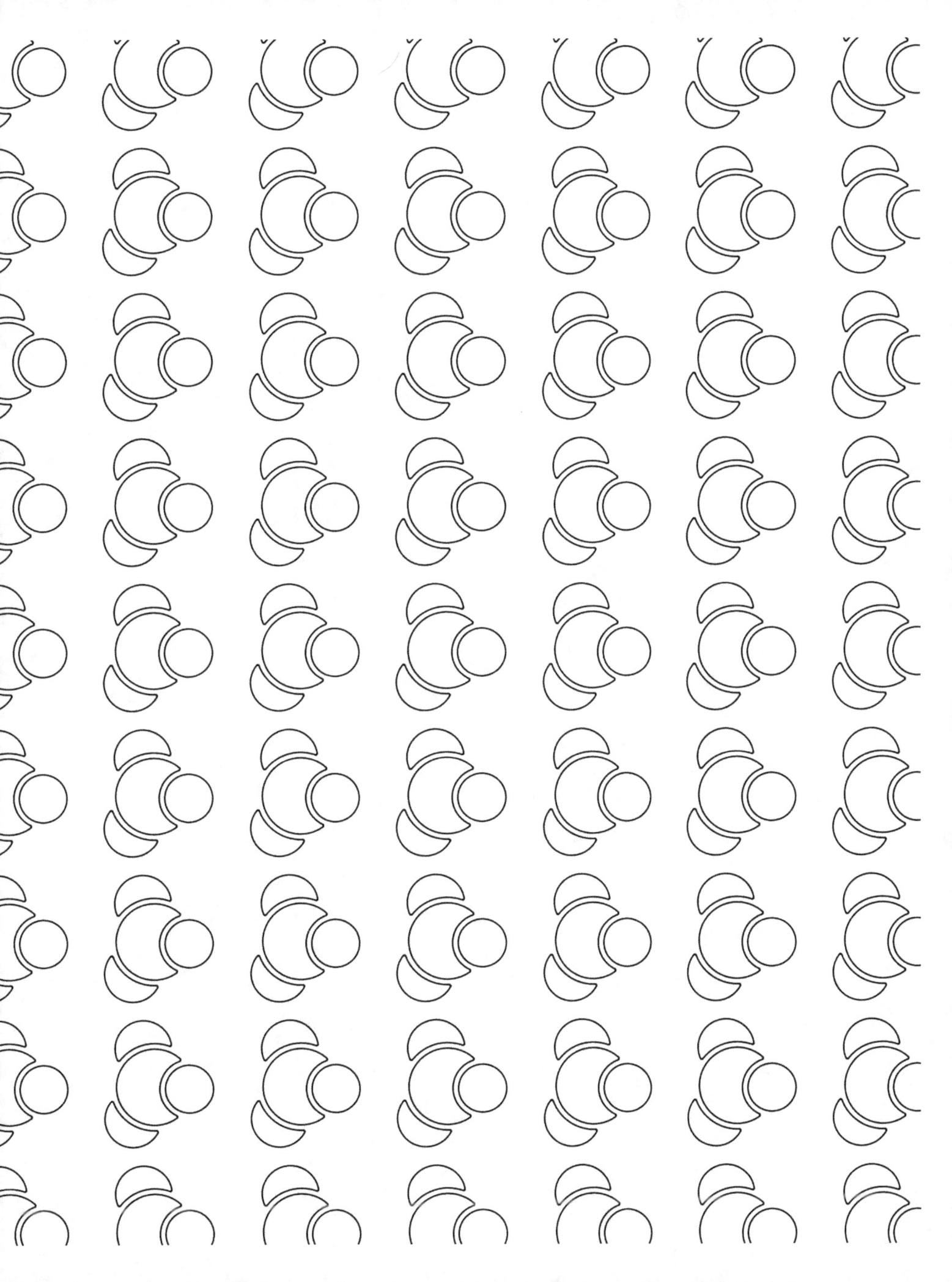

Doodles

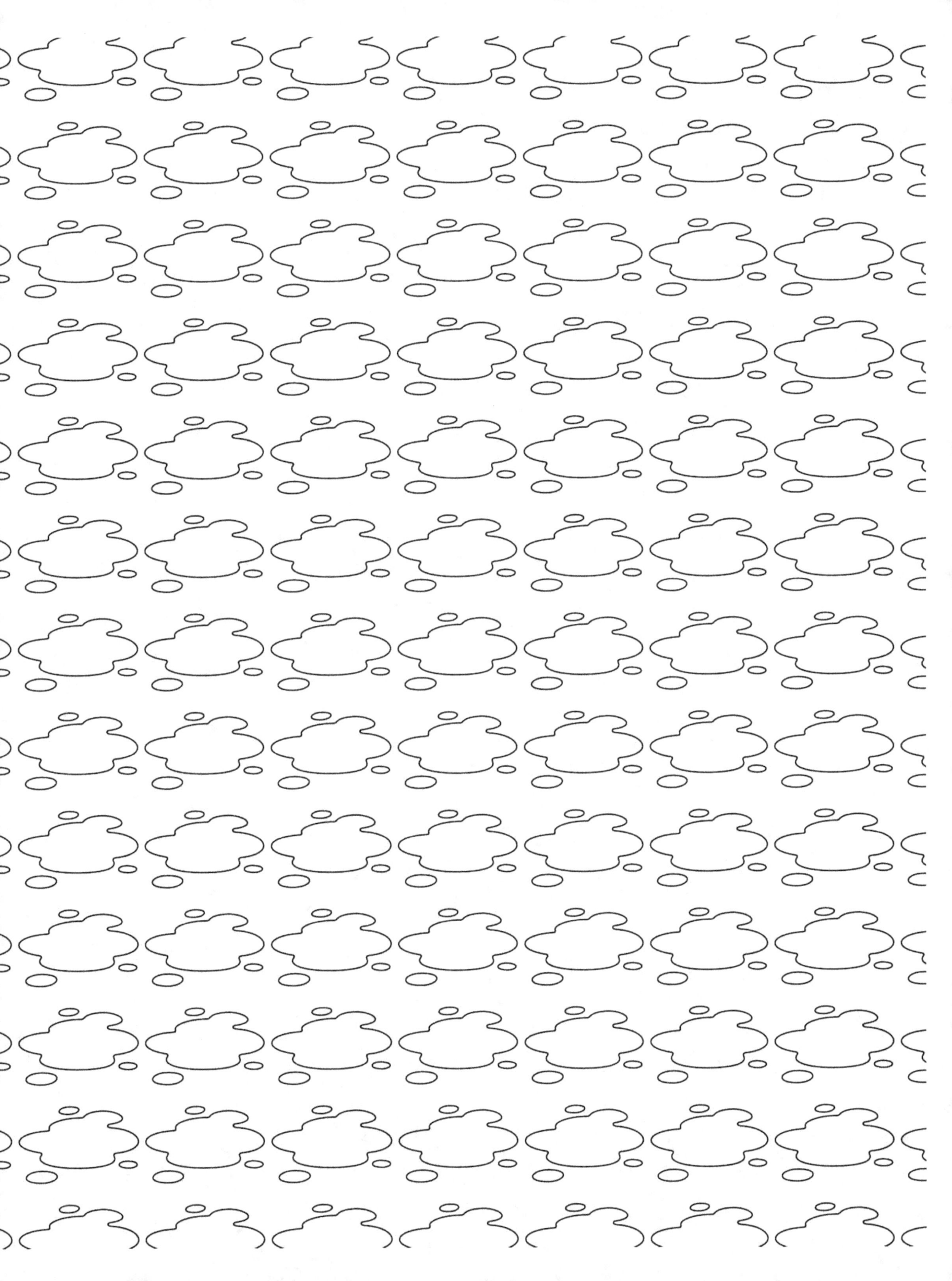

Doodles

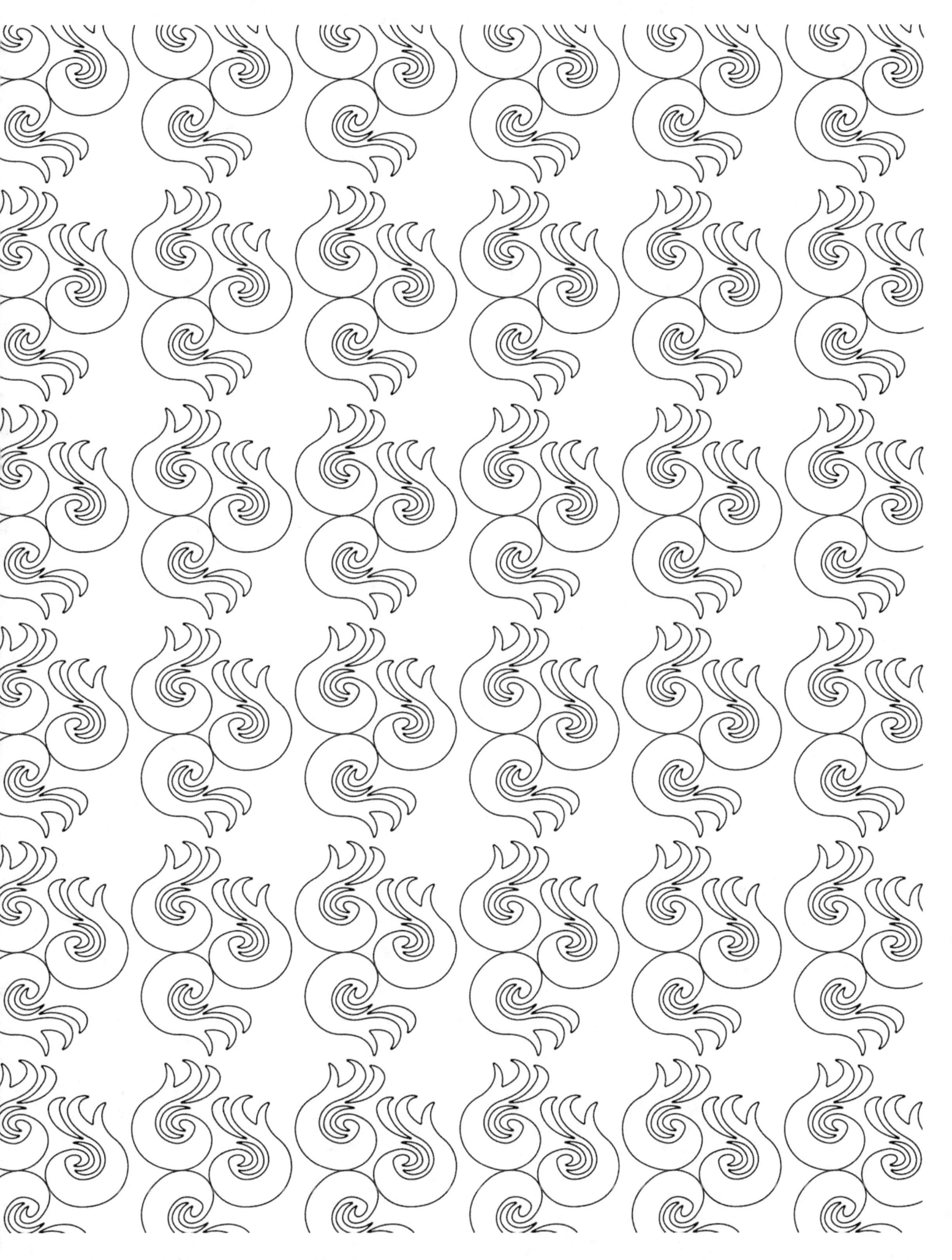

Doodles

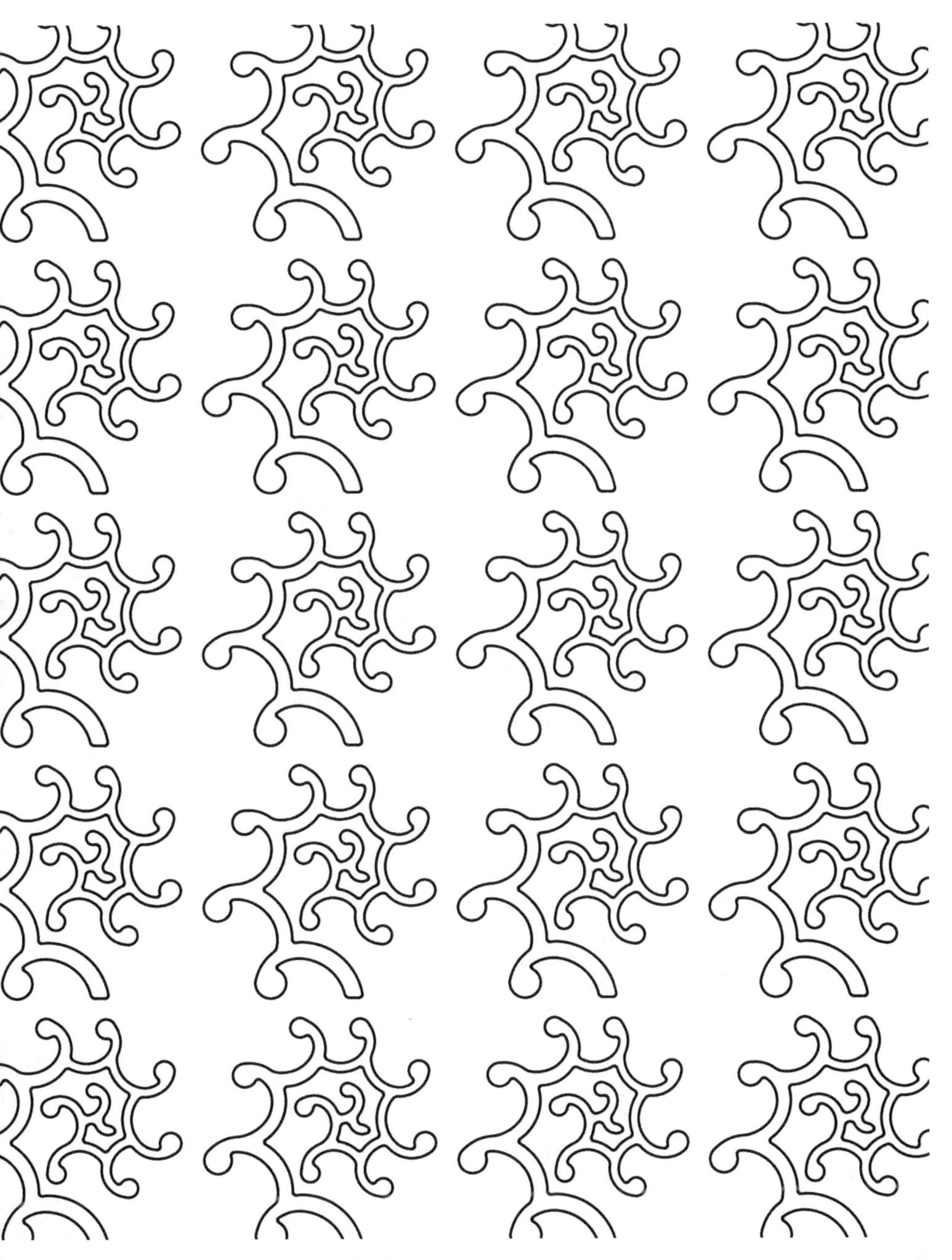

Doodles

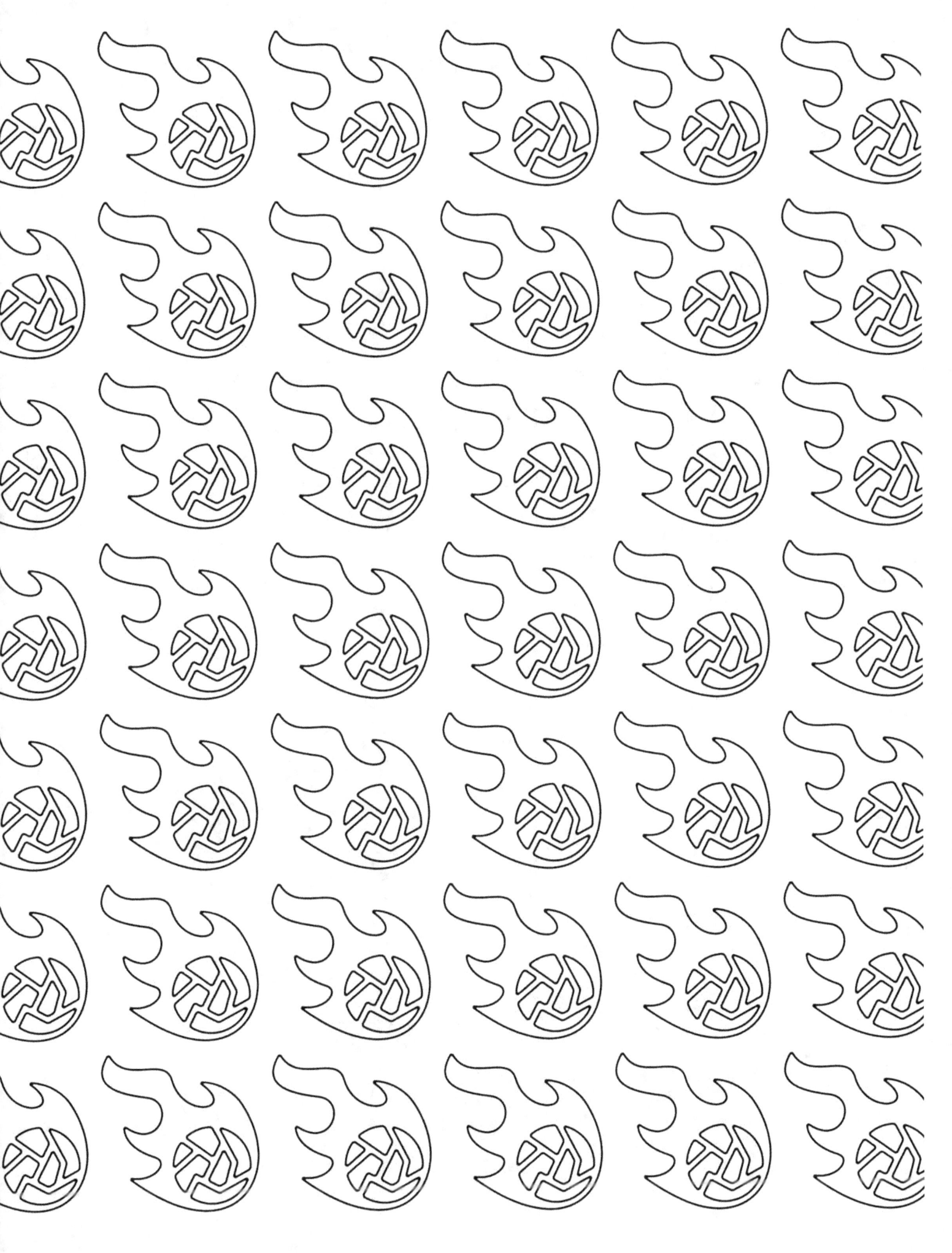

Doodles

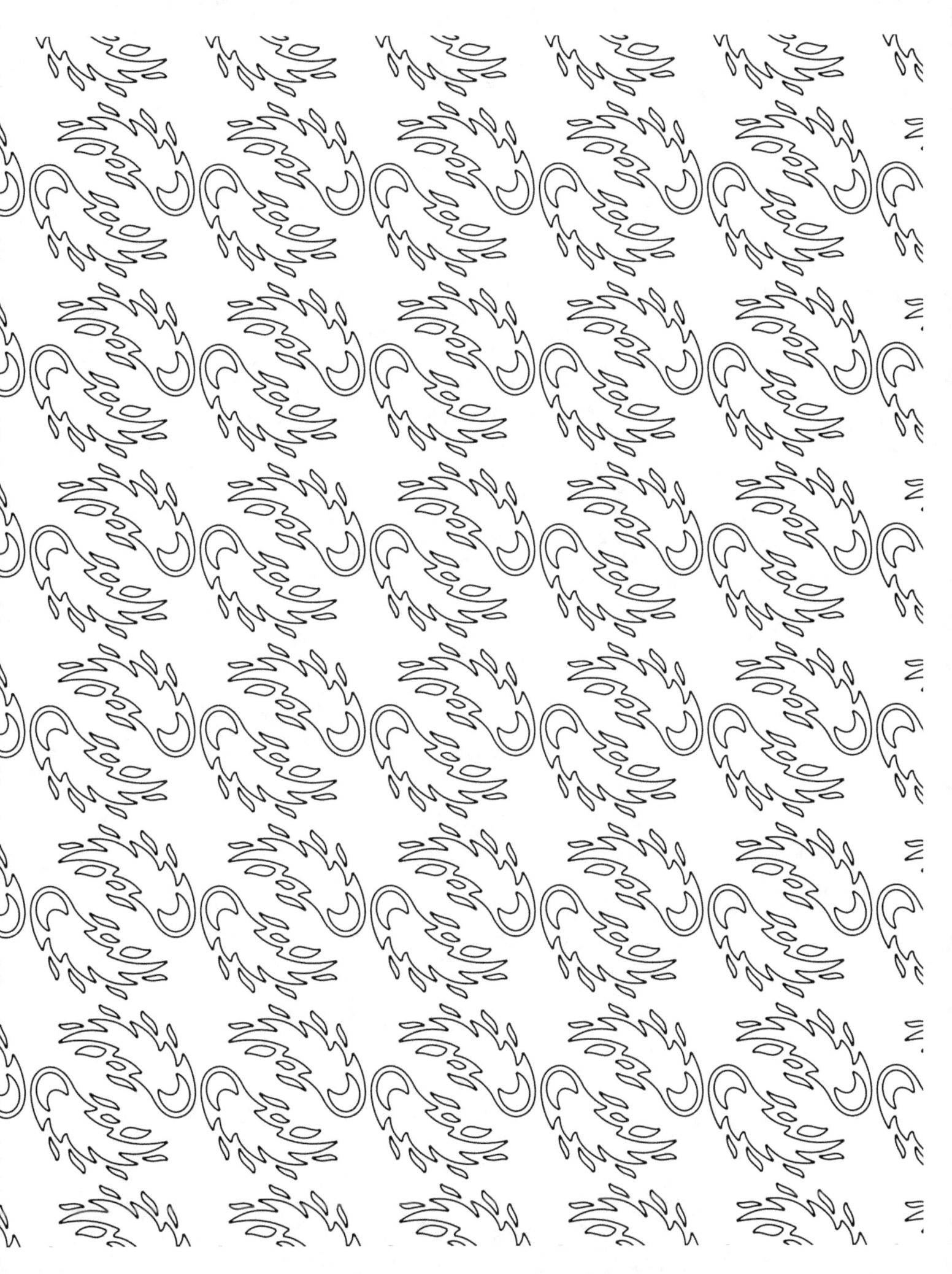

Doodles

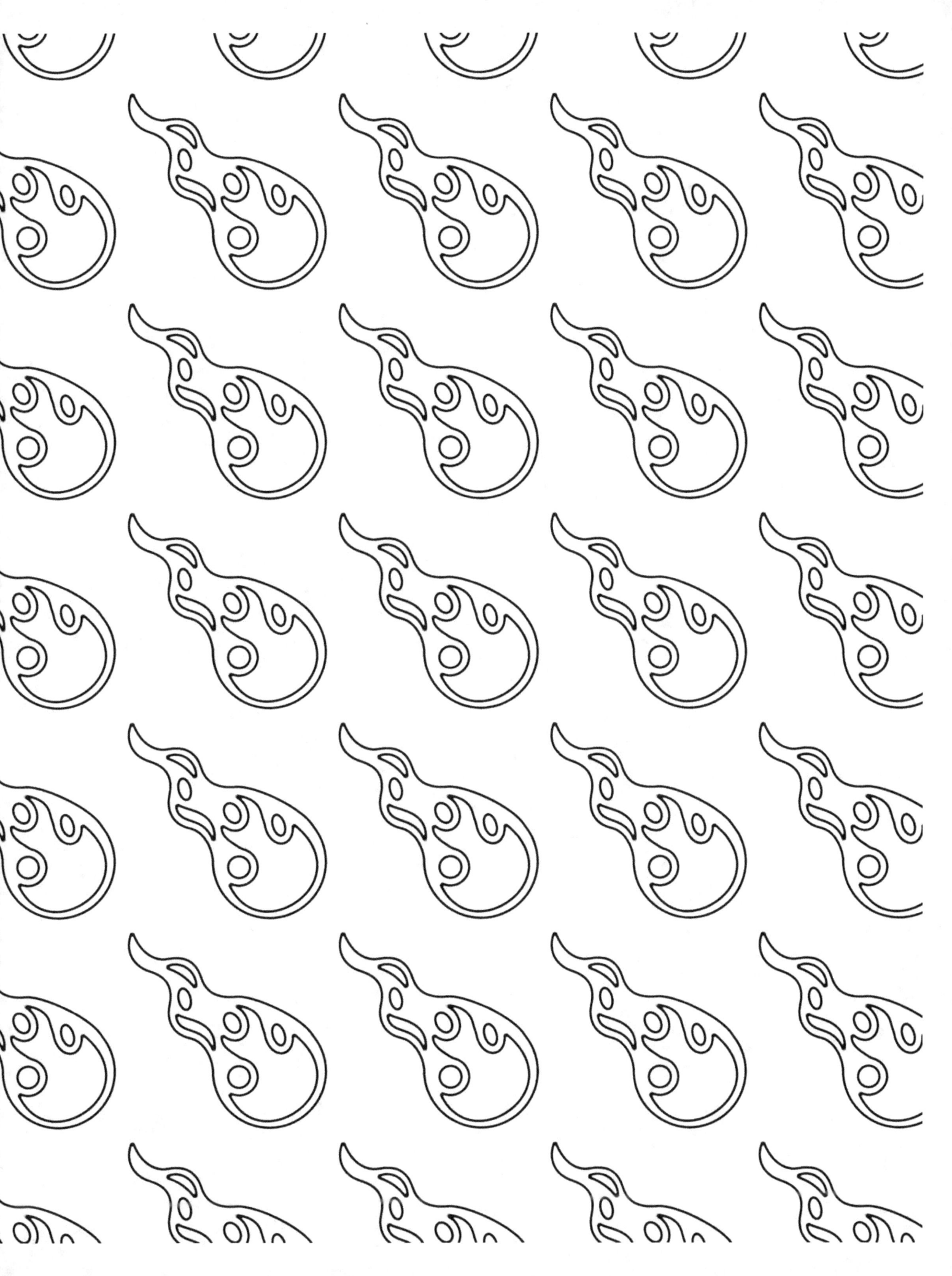

Doodles

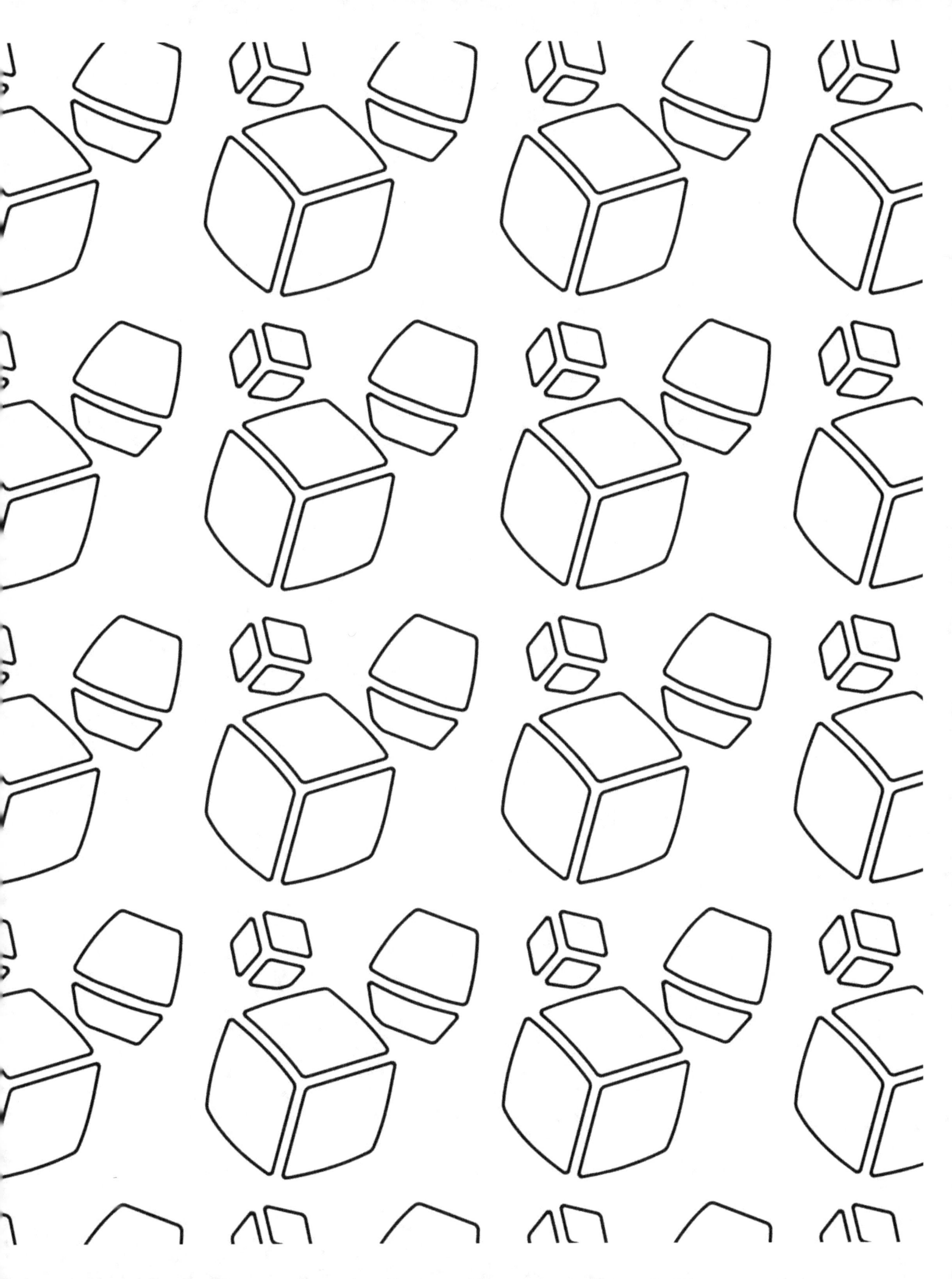

Doodles

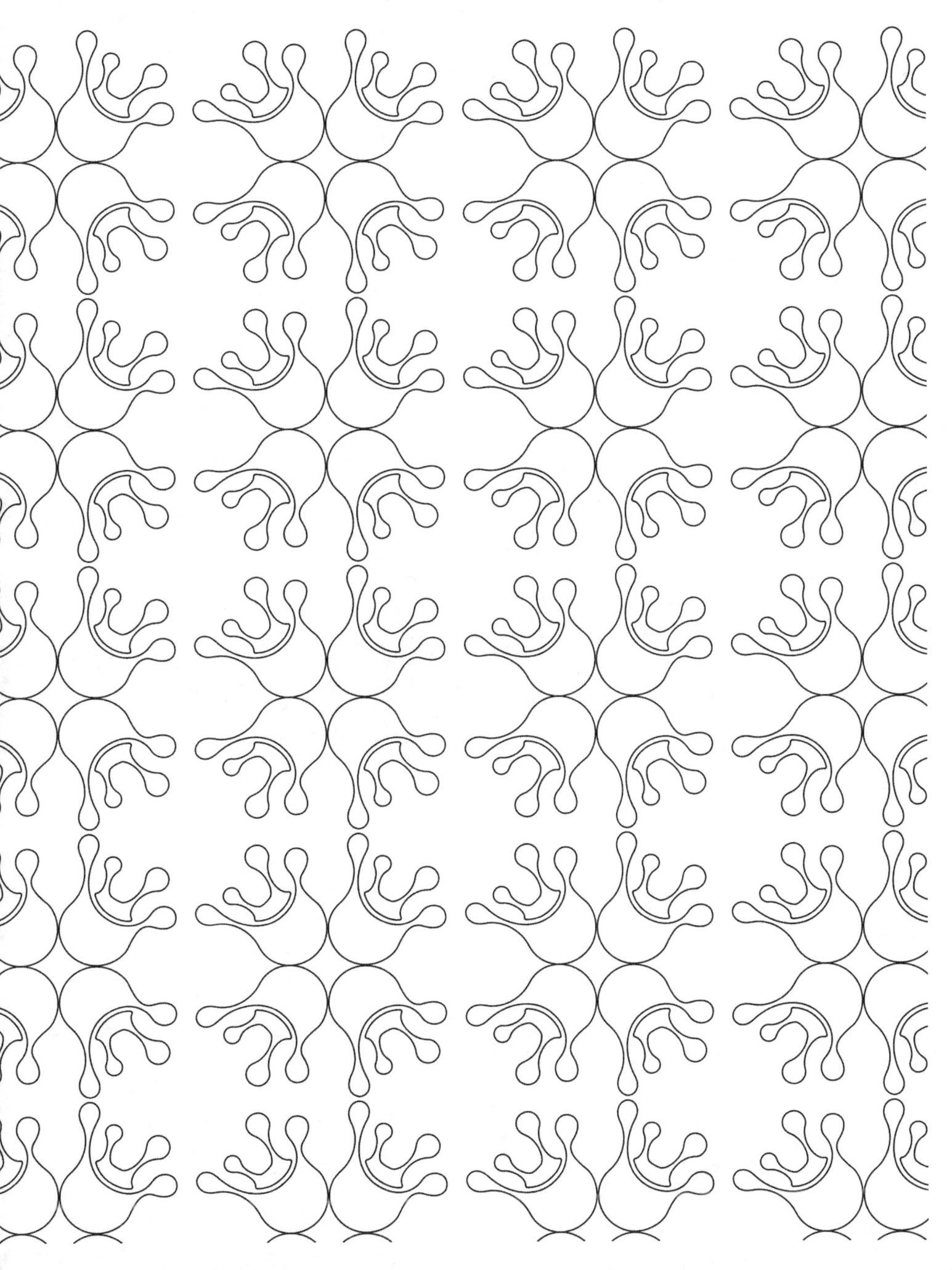

Doodles

Doodles

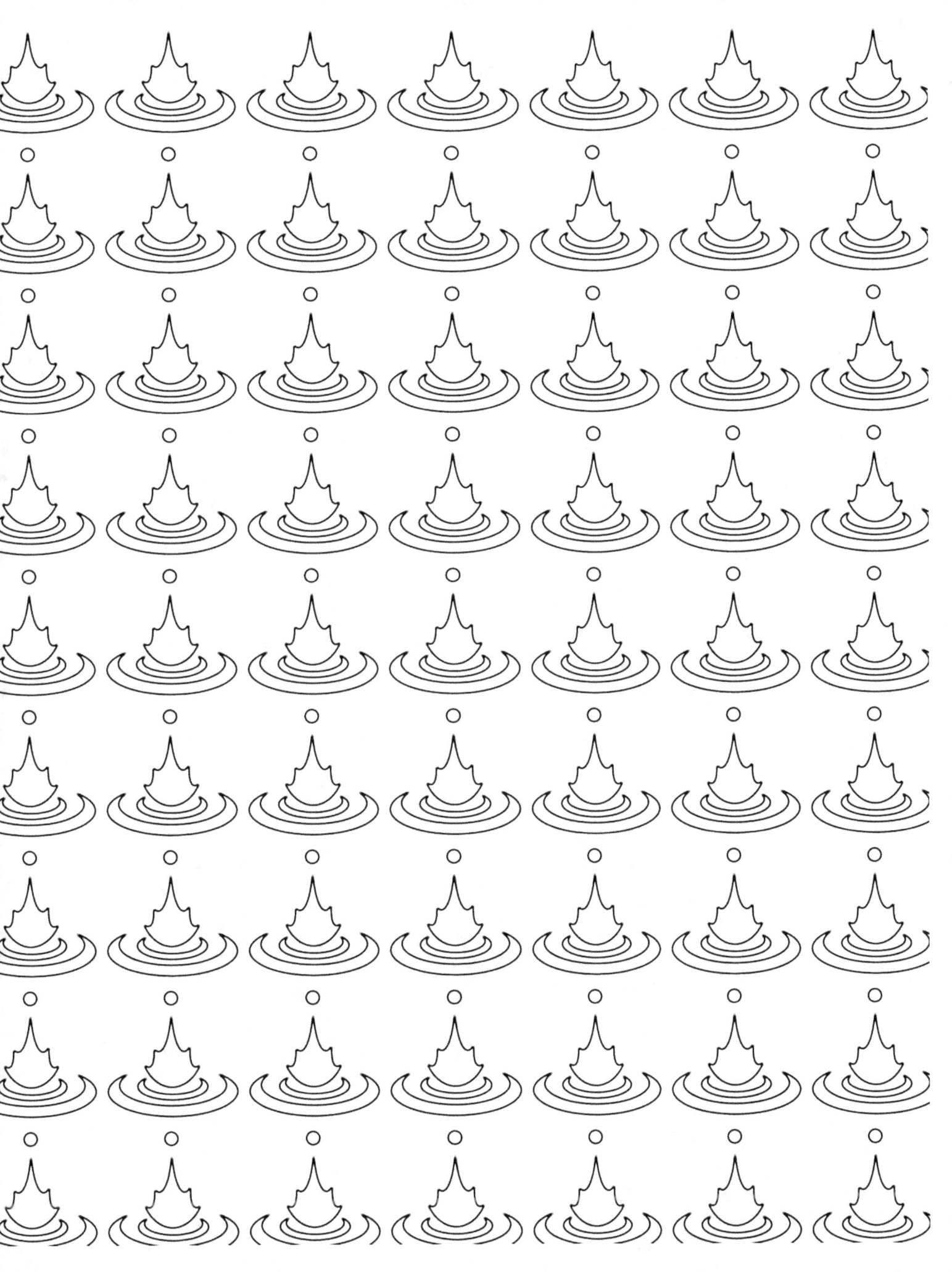

Doodles

Doodles

Doodles

Doodles

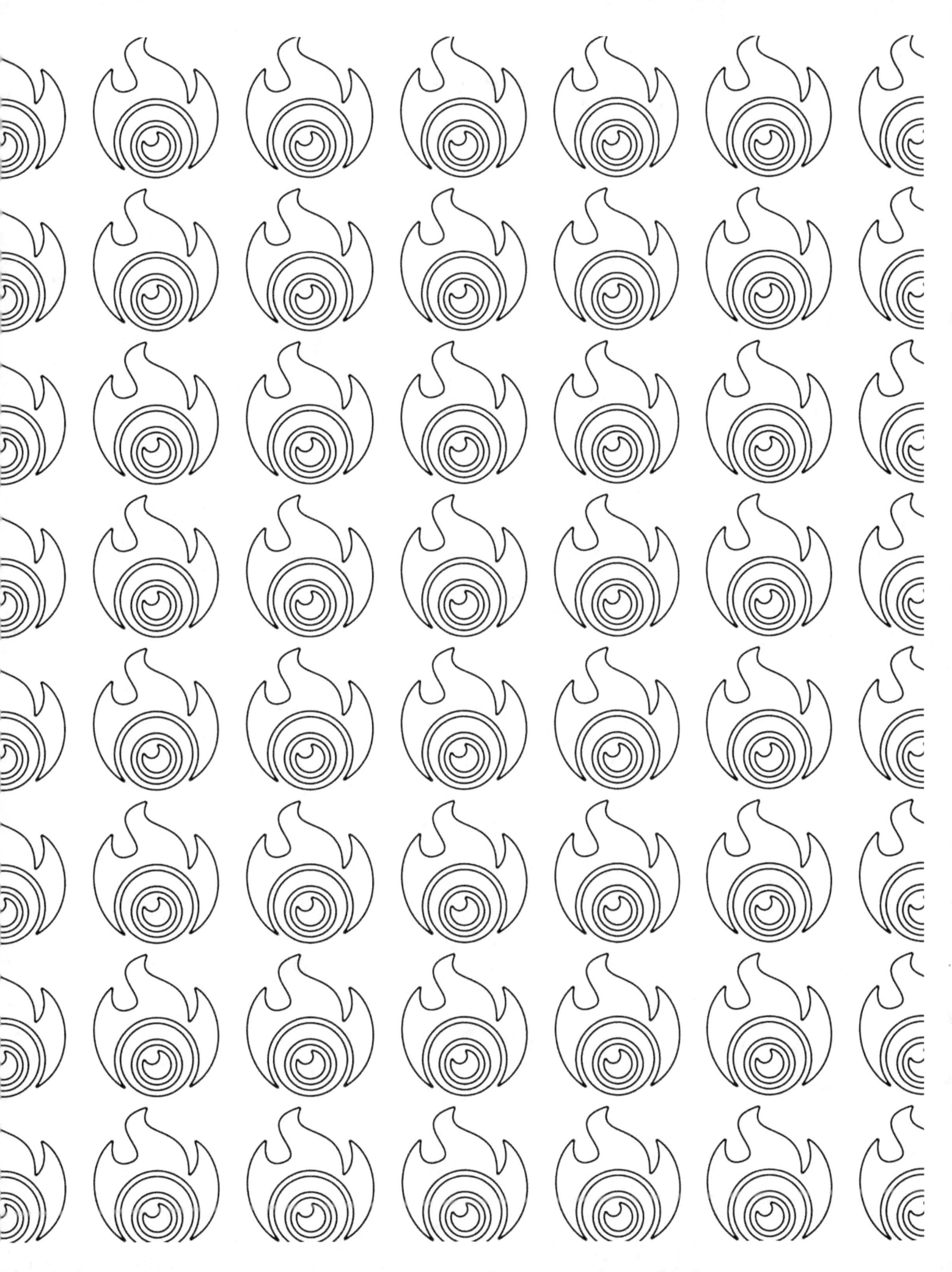

Doodles

Doodles

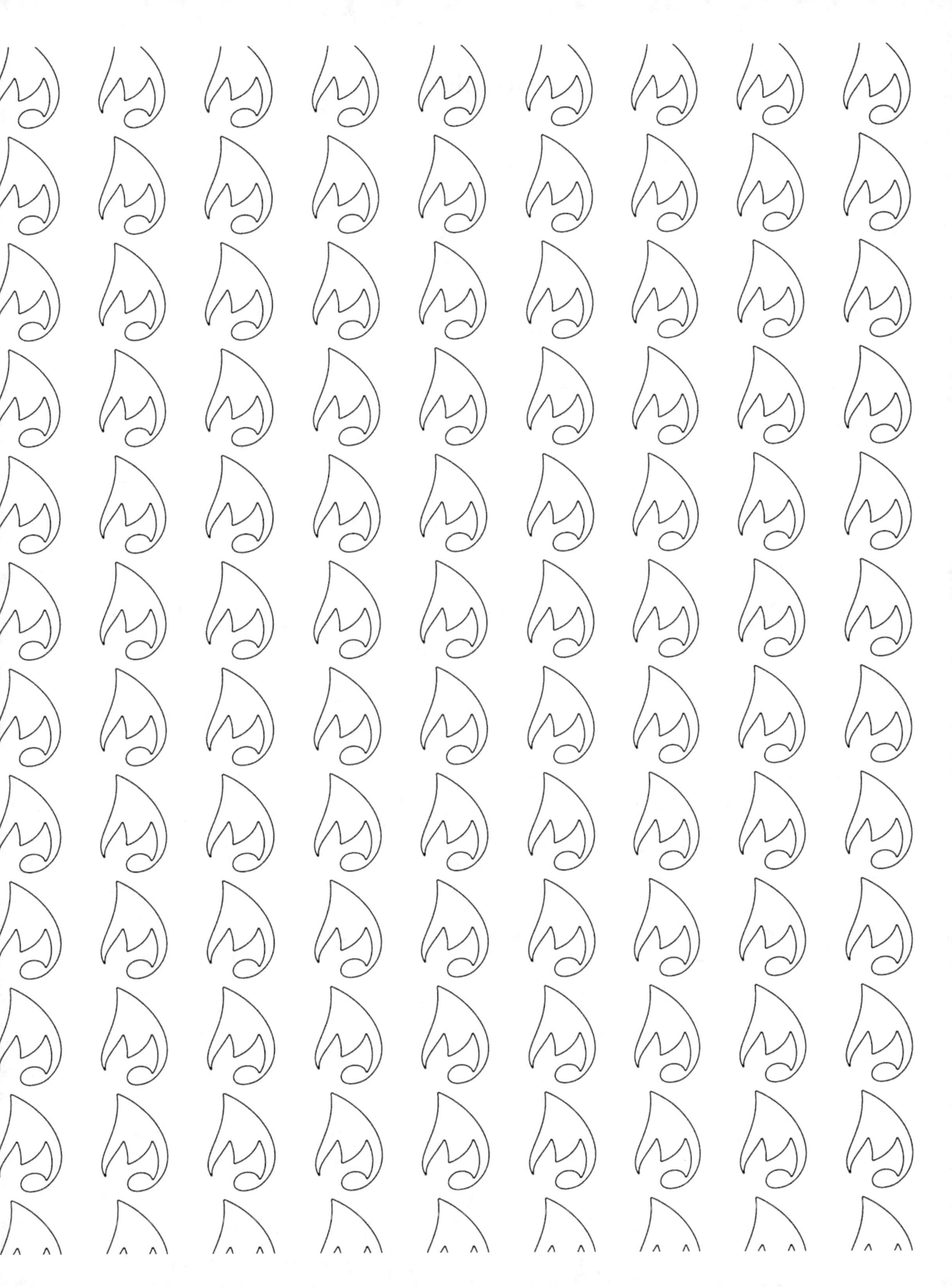

Doodles

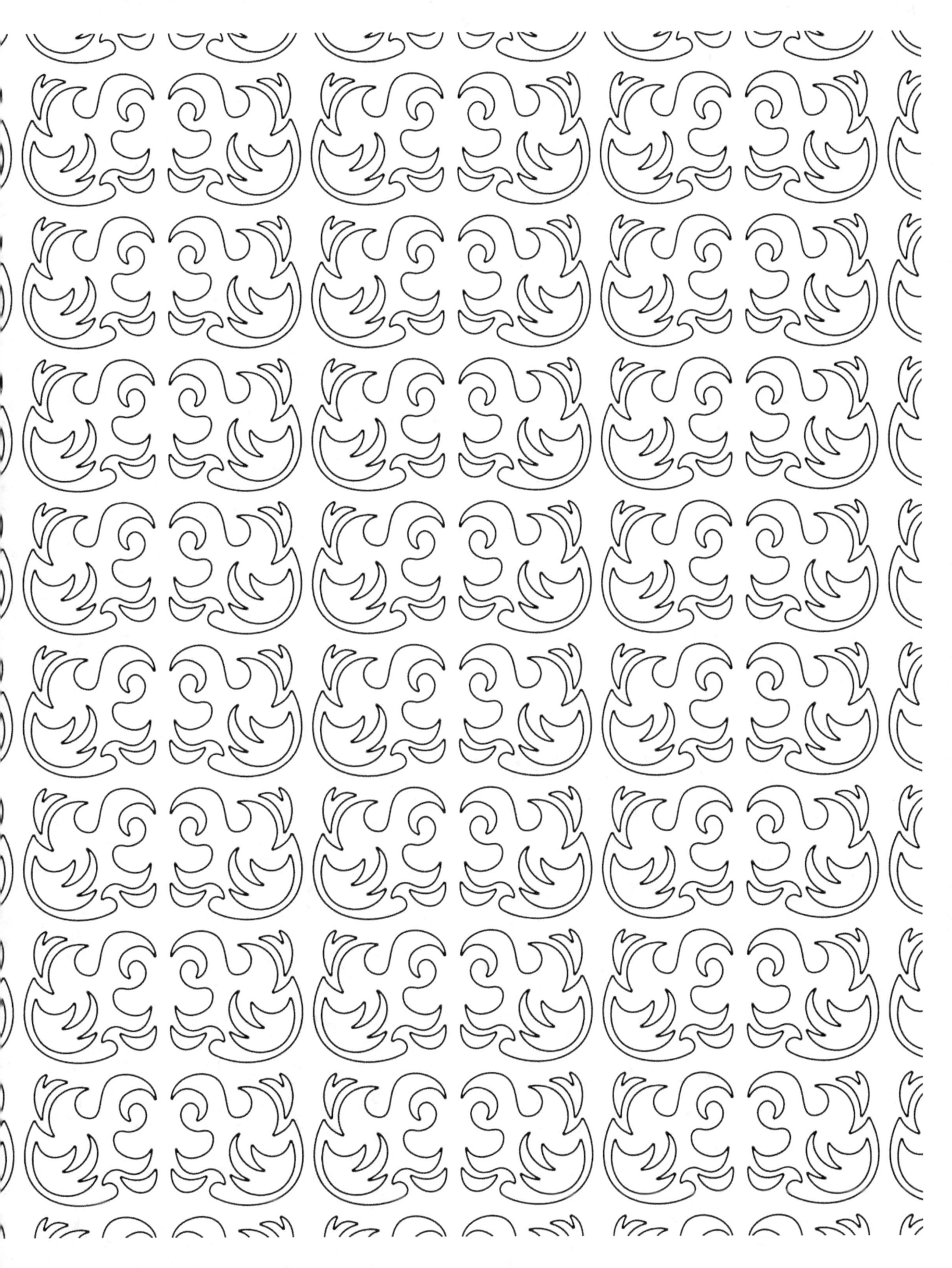

Doodles

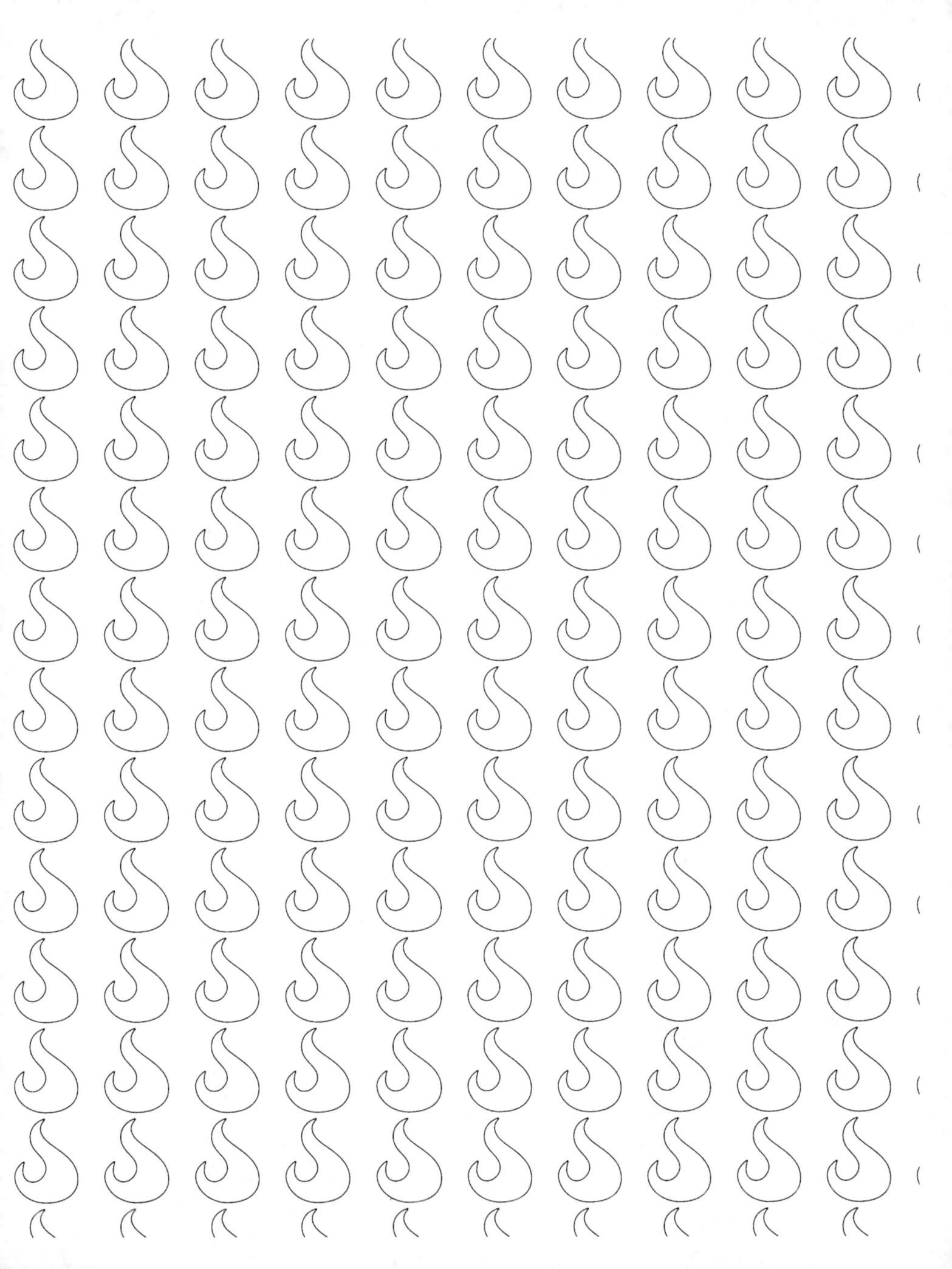

Doodles

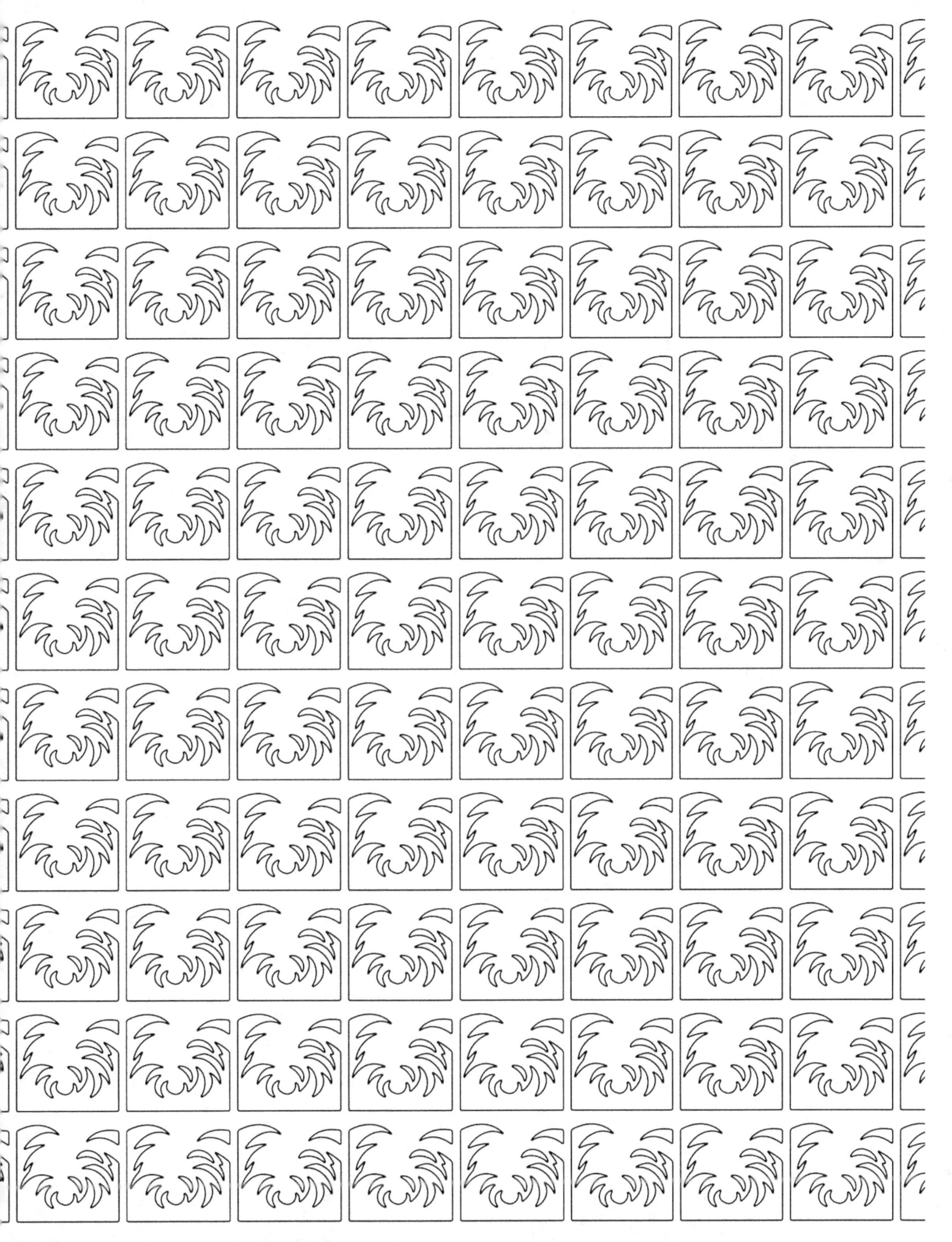

Doodles

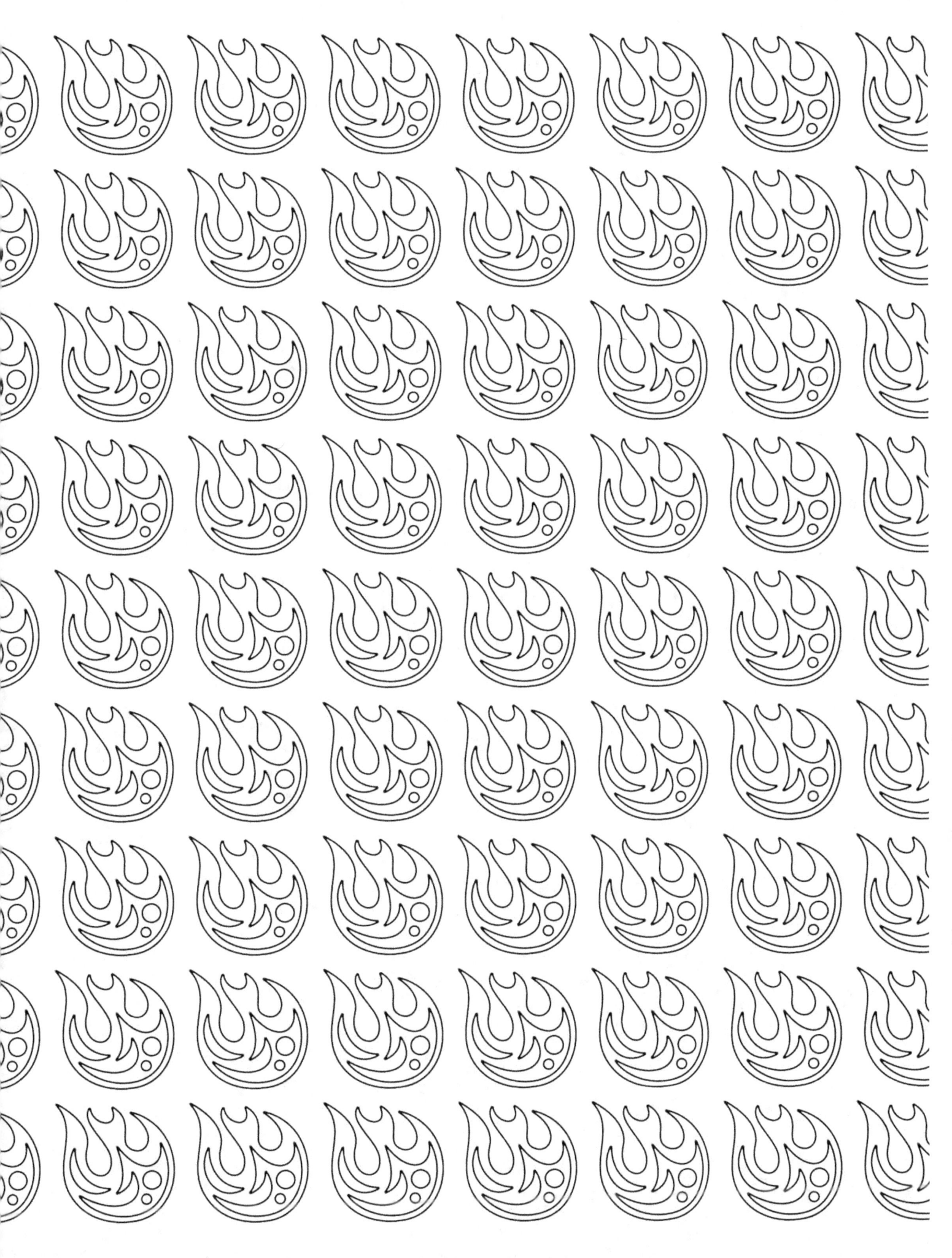

Doodles

Doodles

Doodles

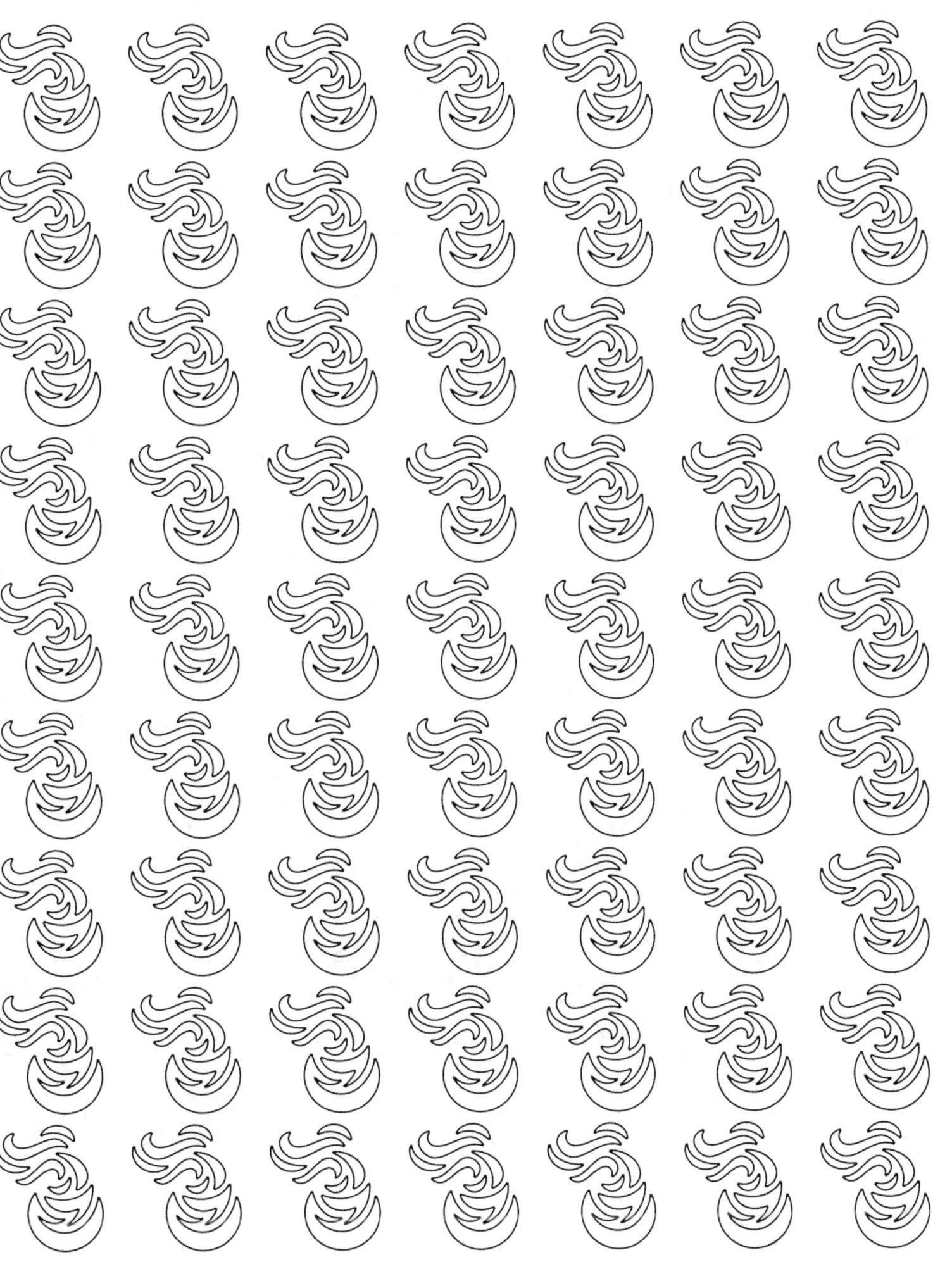

Doodles

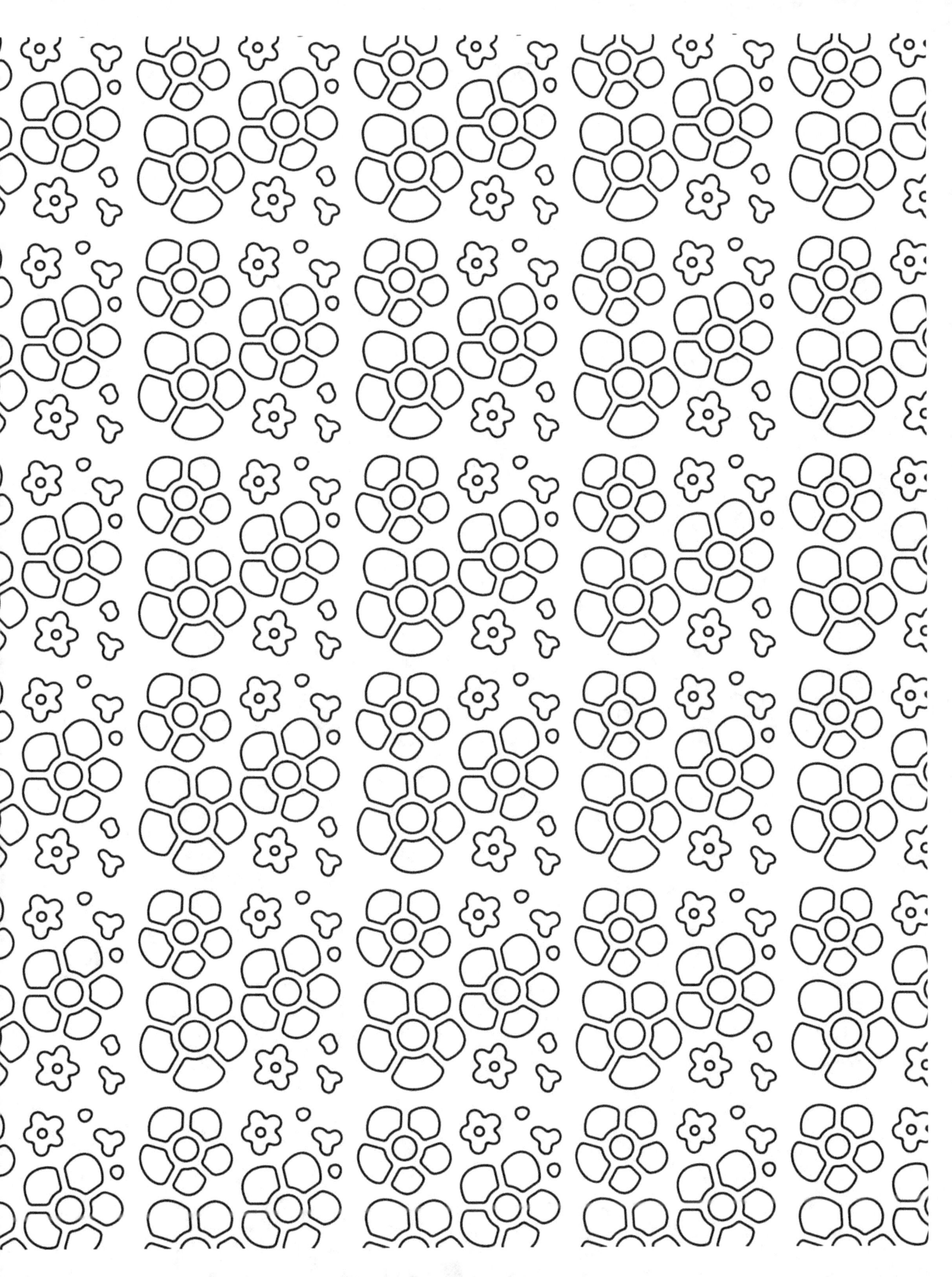

Doodles

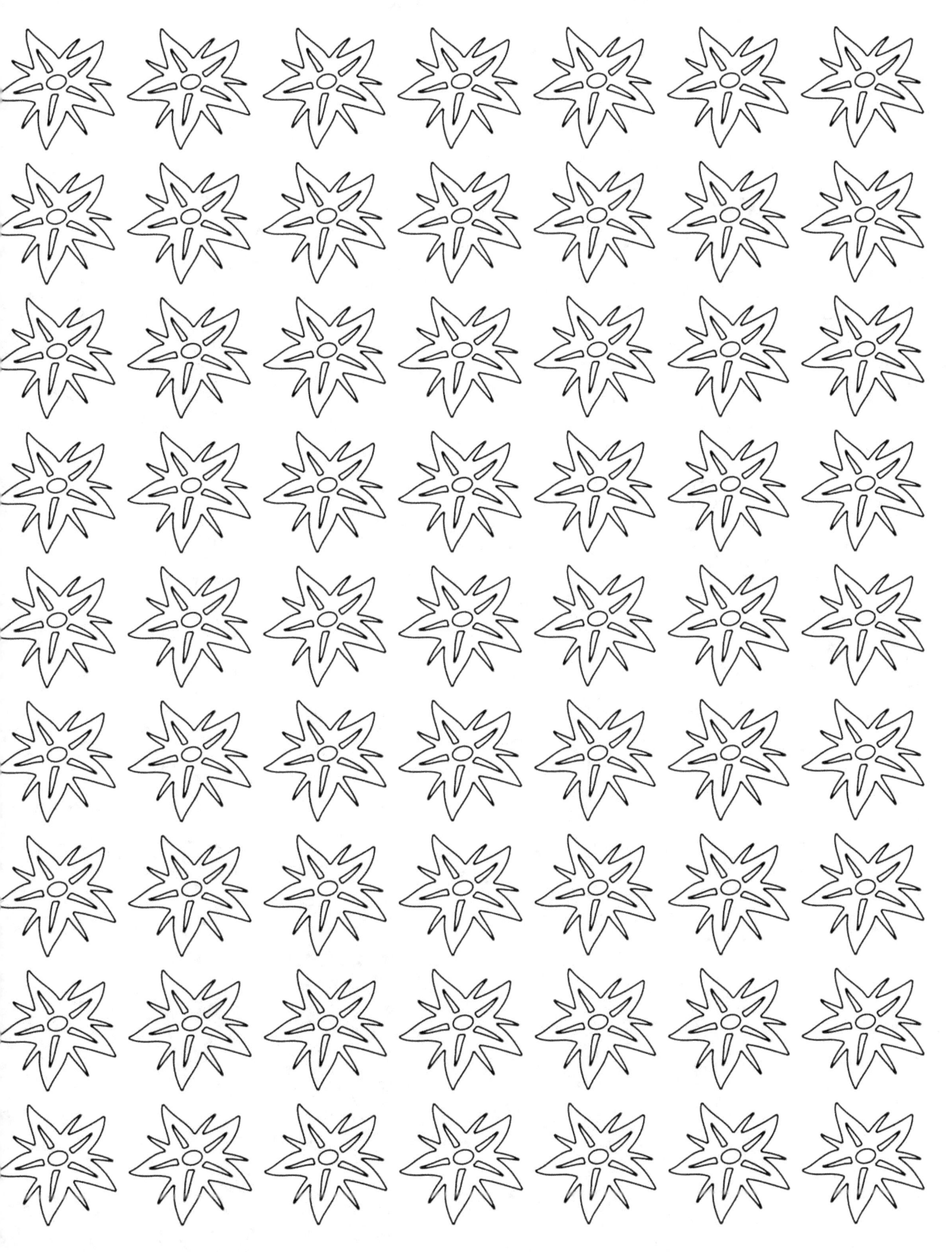

Doodles

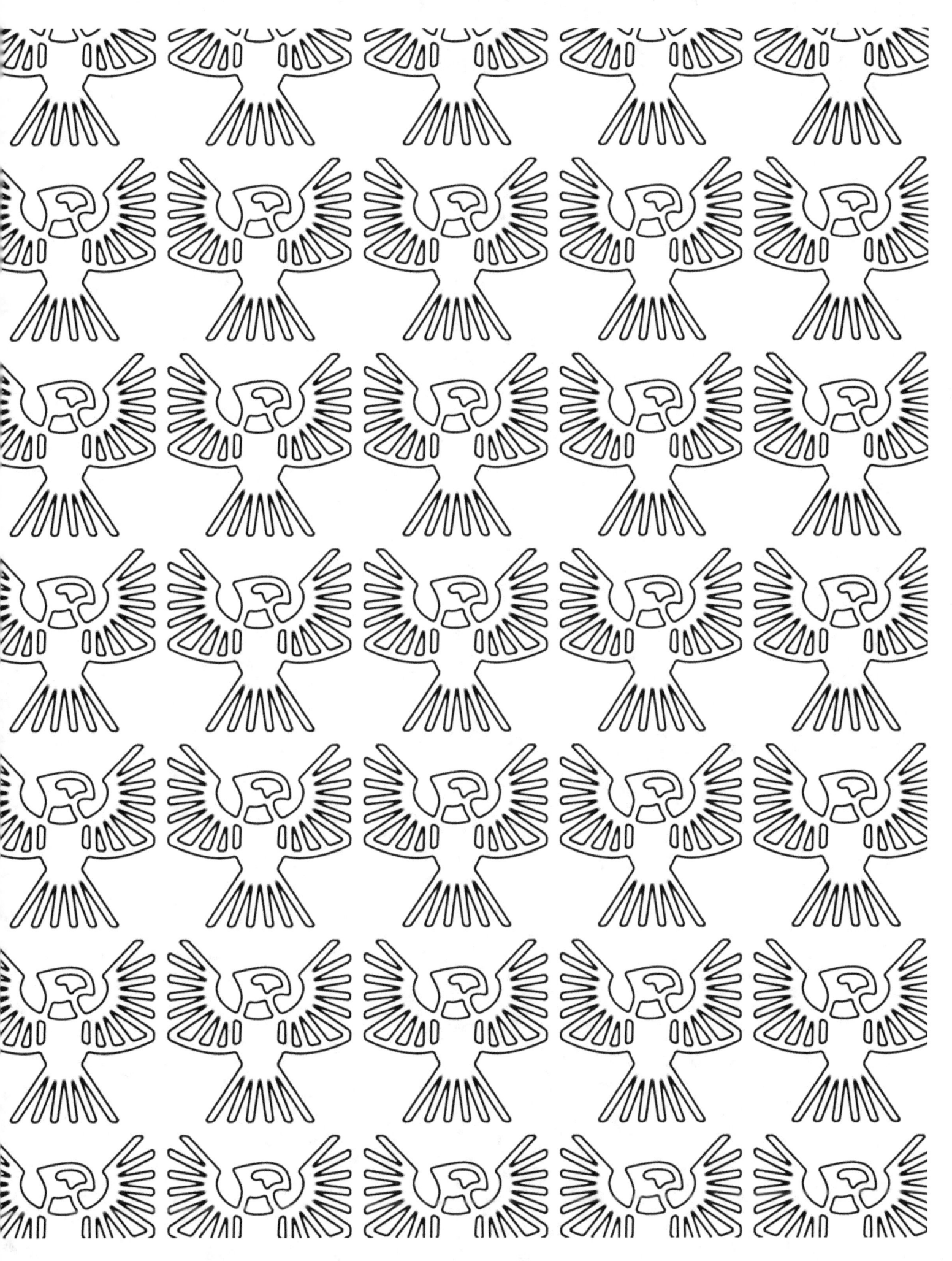

Doodles

Doodles

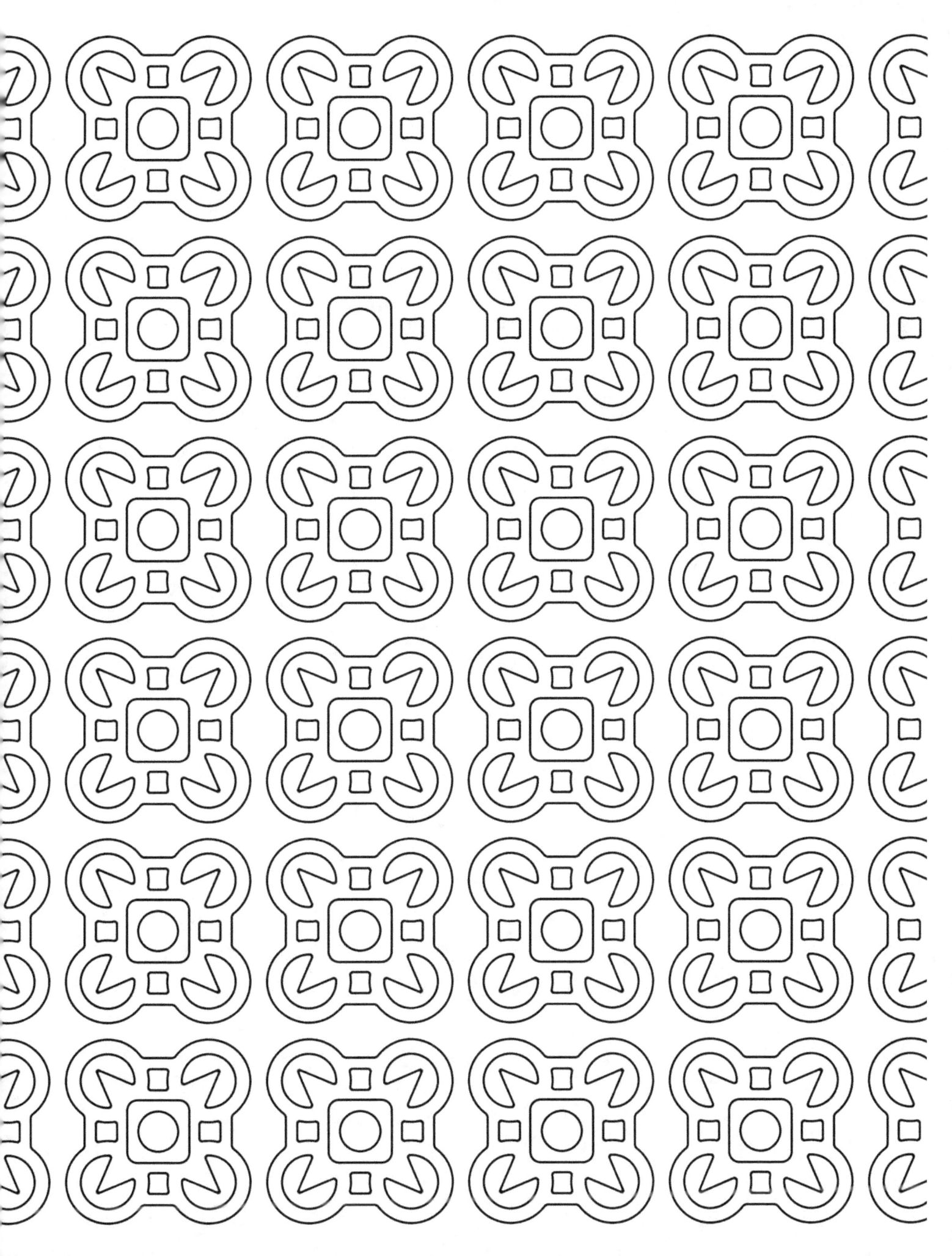

Doodles

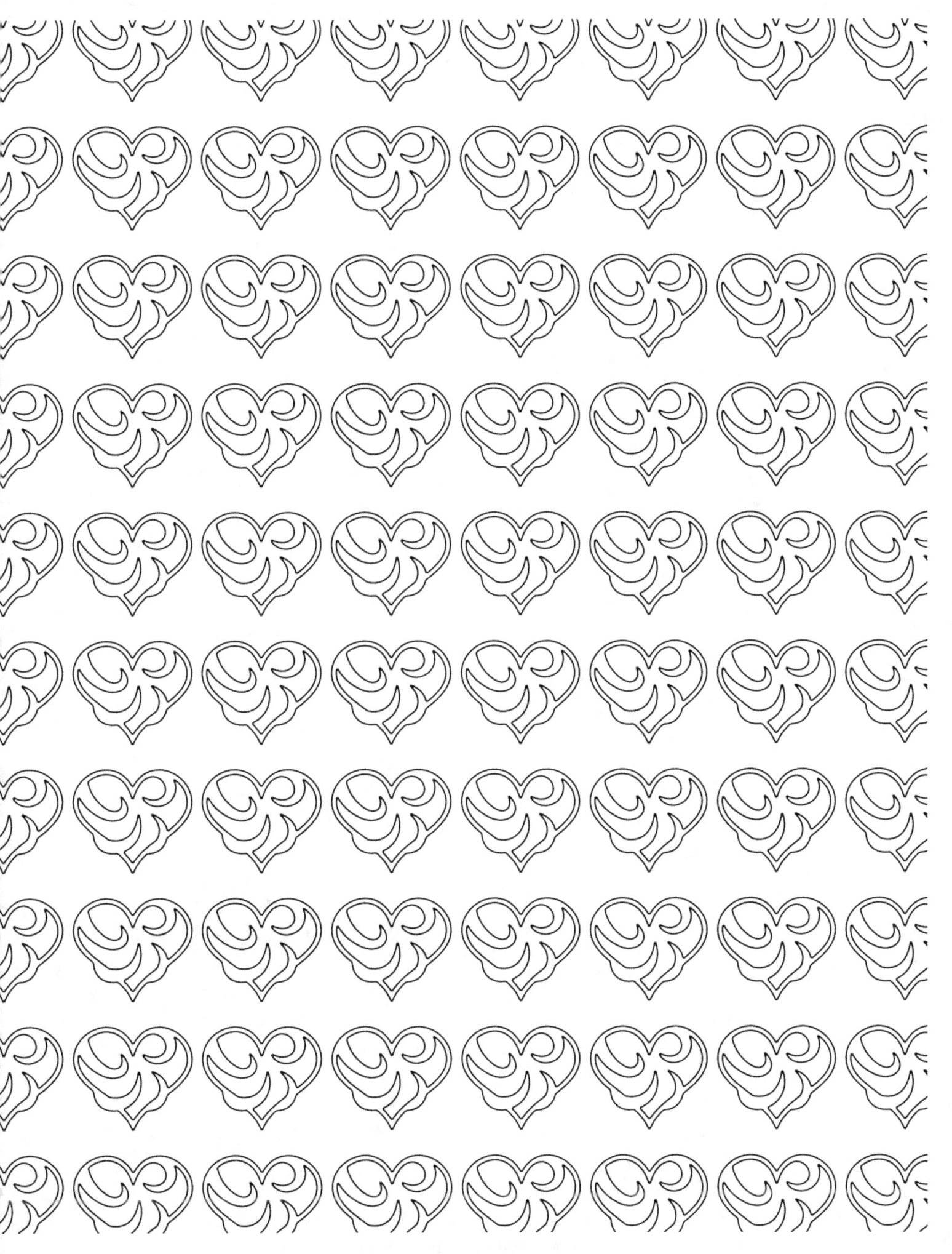

Doodles

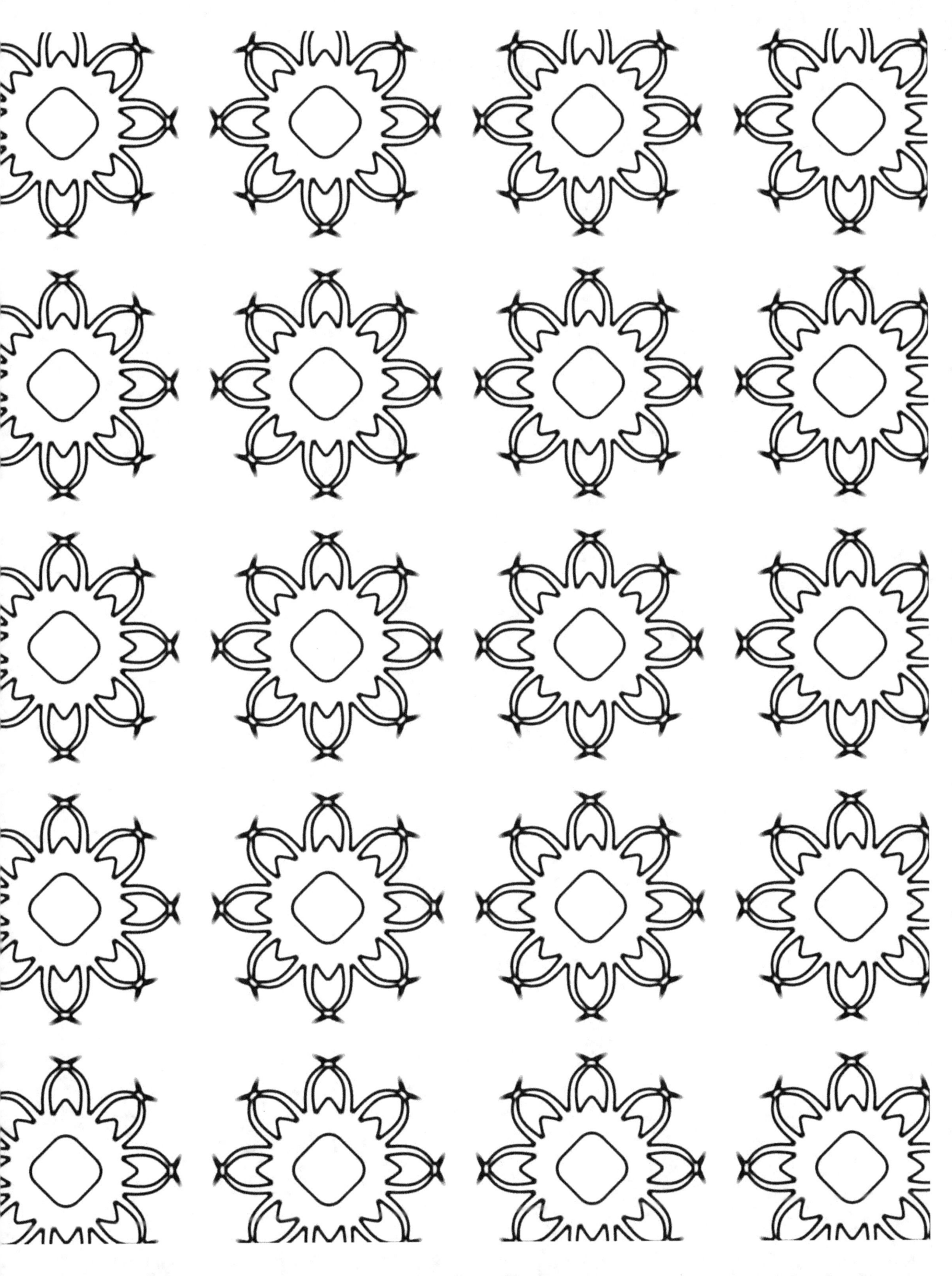

Doodles

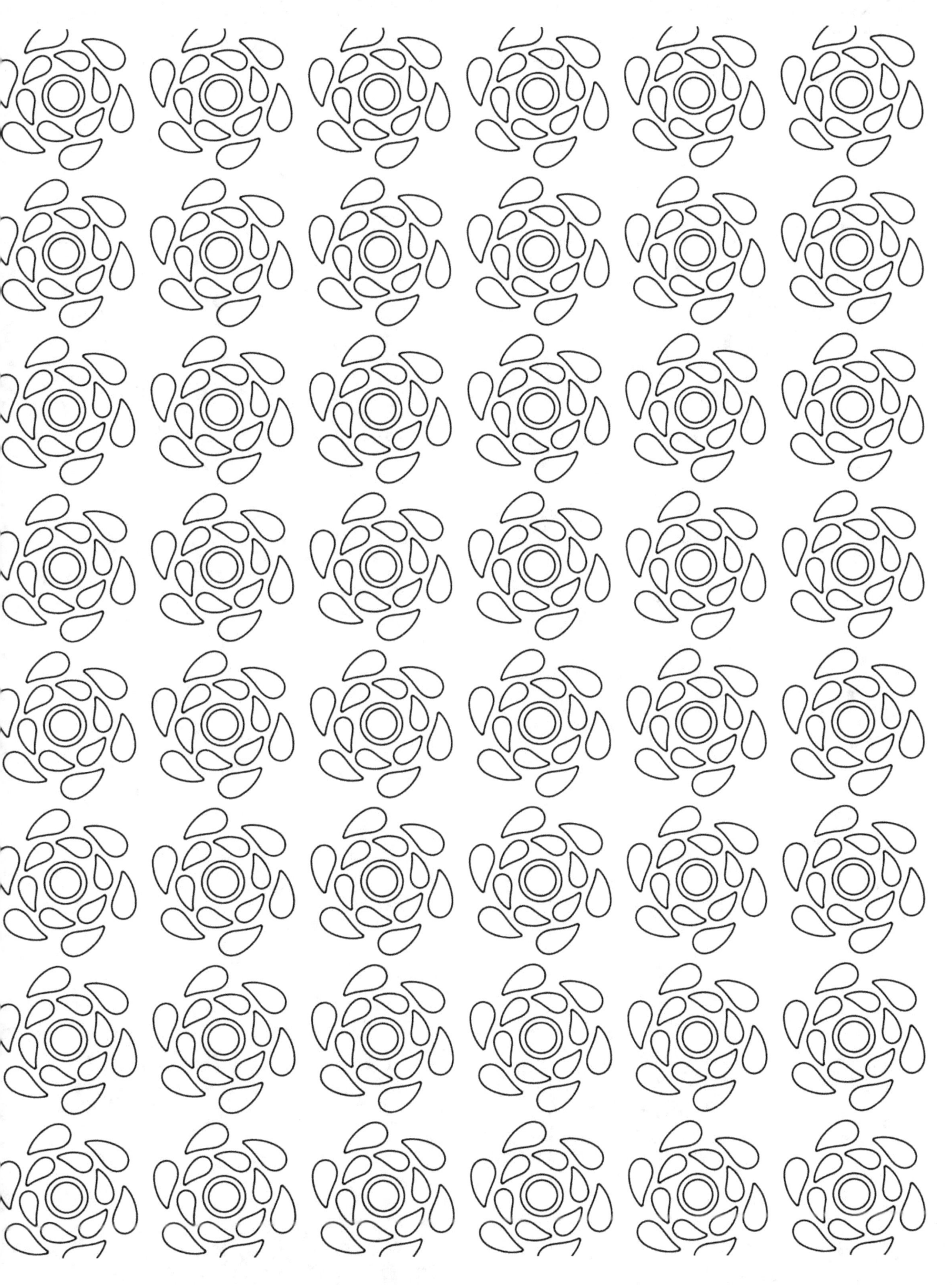

Doodles

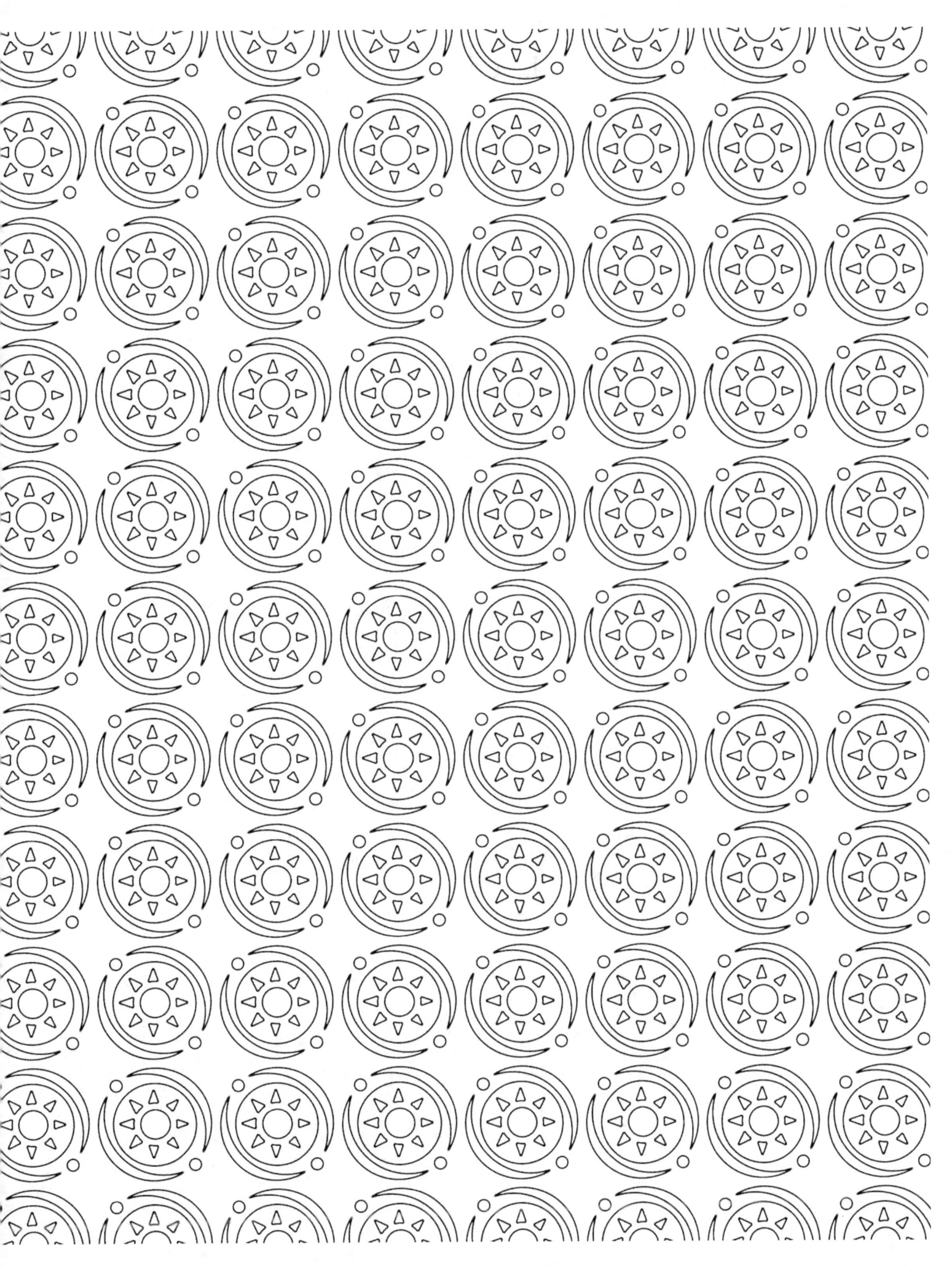

Doodles

Doodles

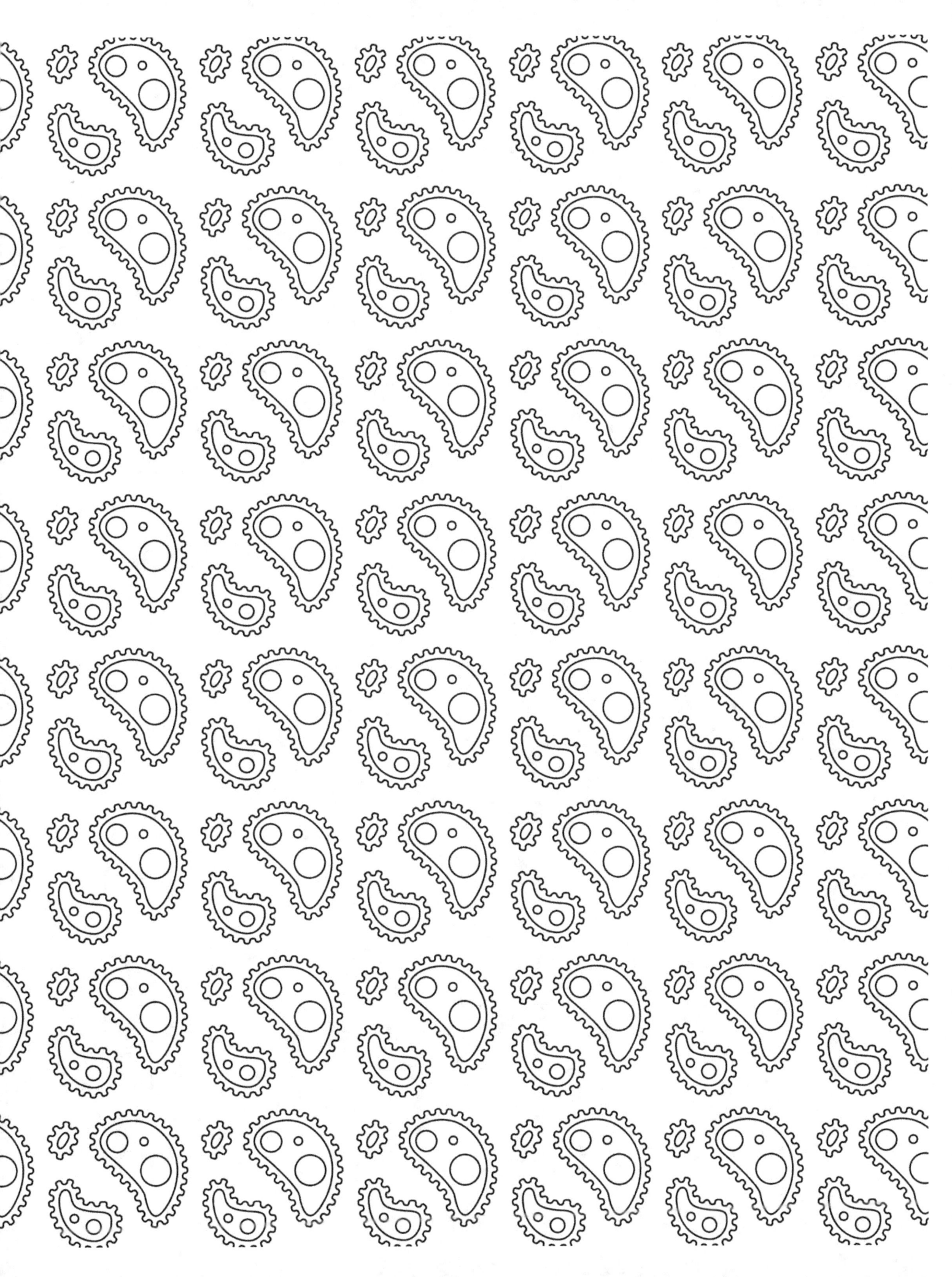

Doodles

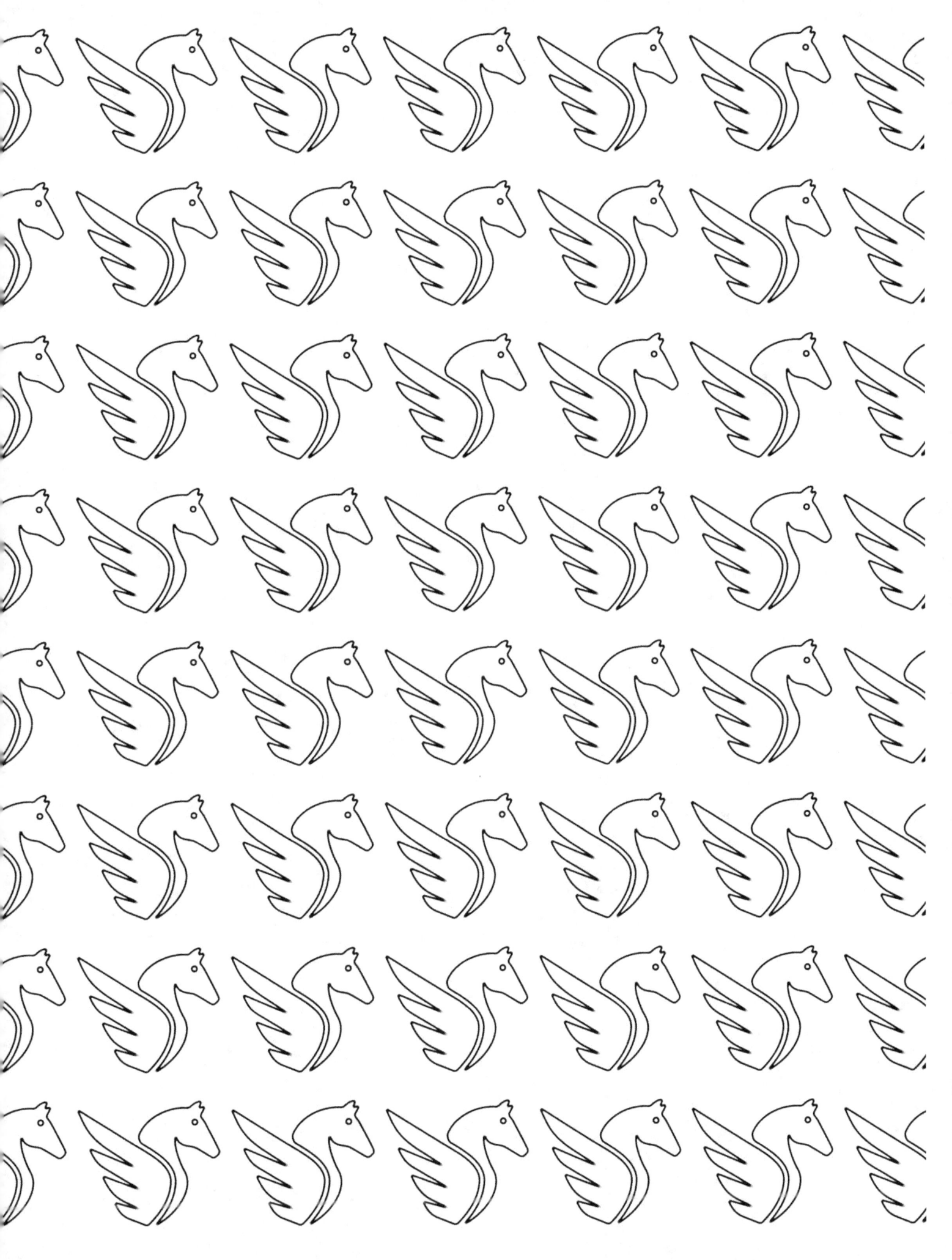

Doodles

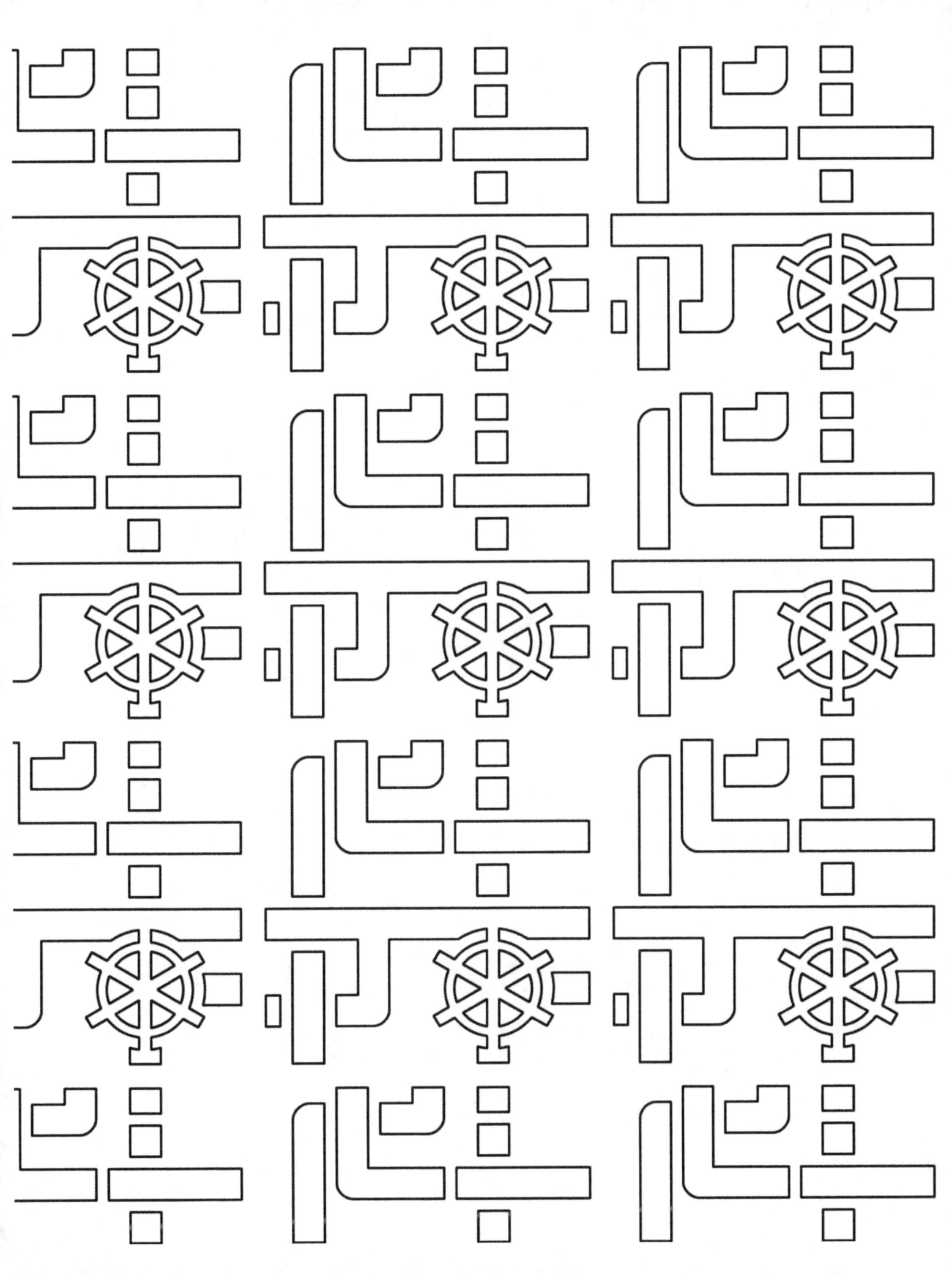

Doodles

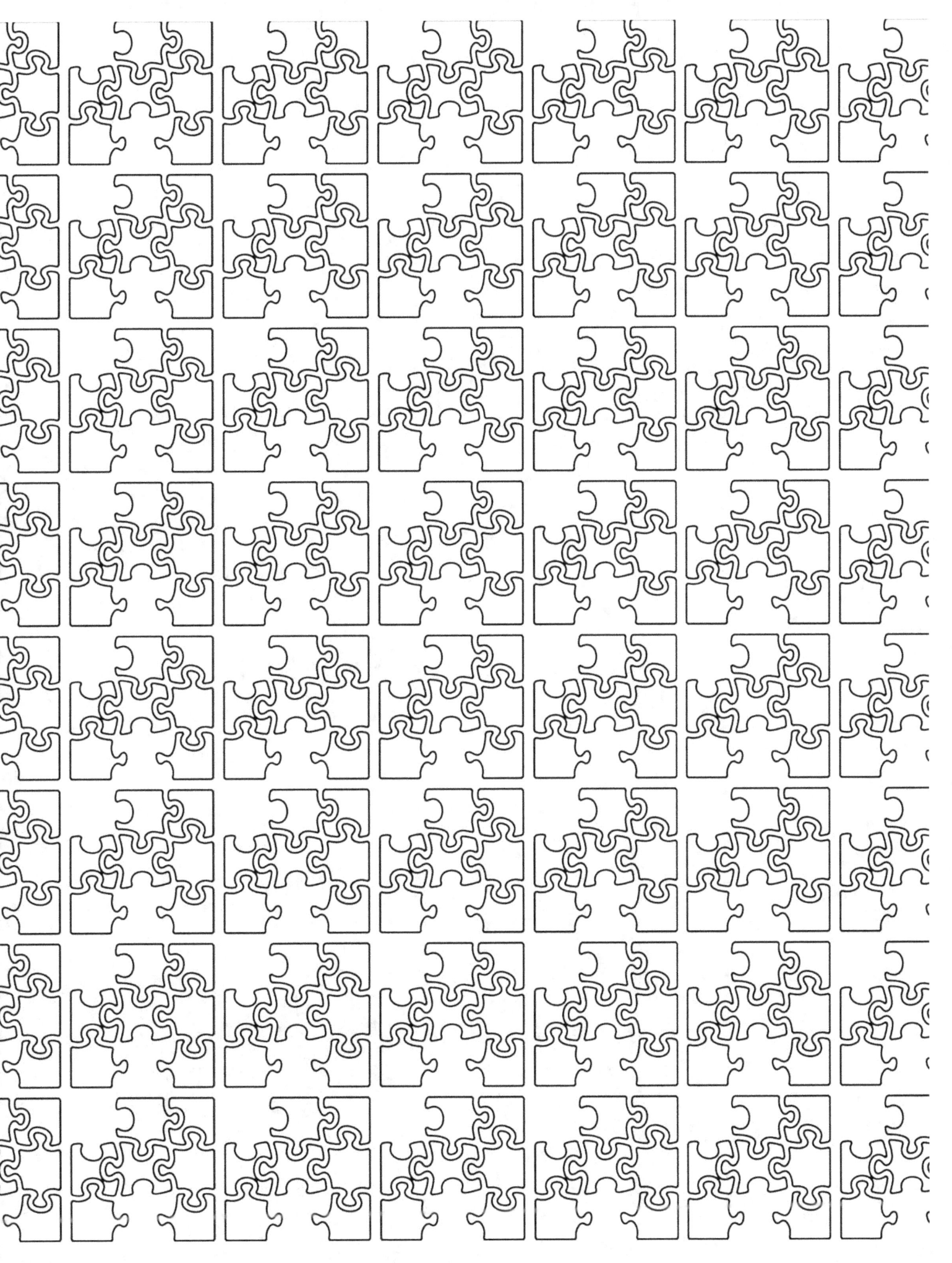

Doodles

Doodles

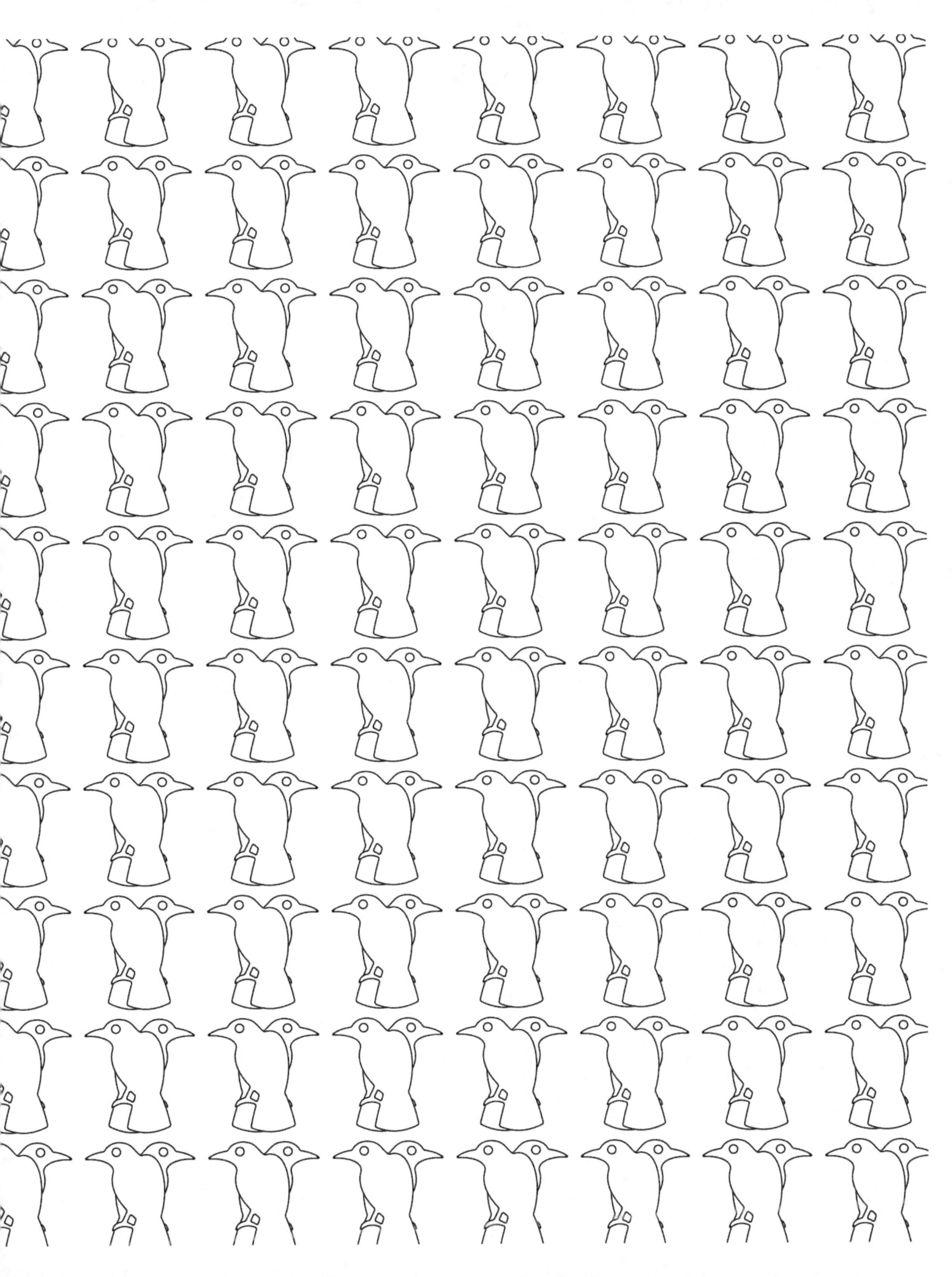

Doodles

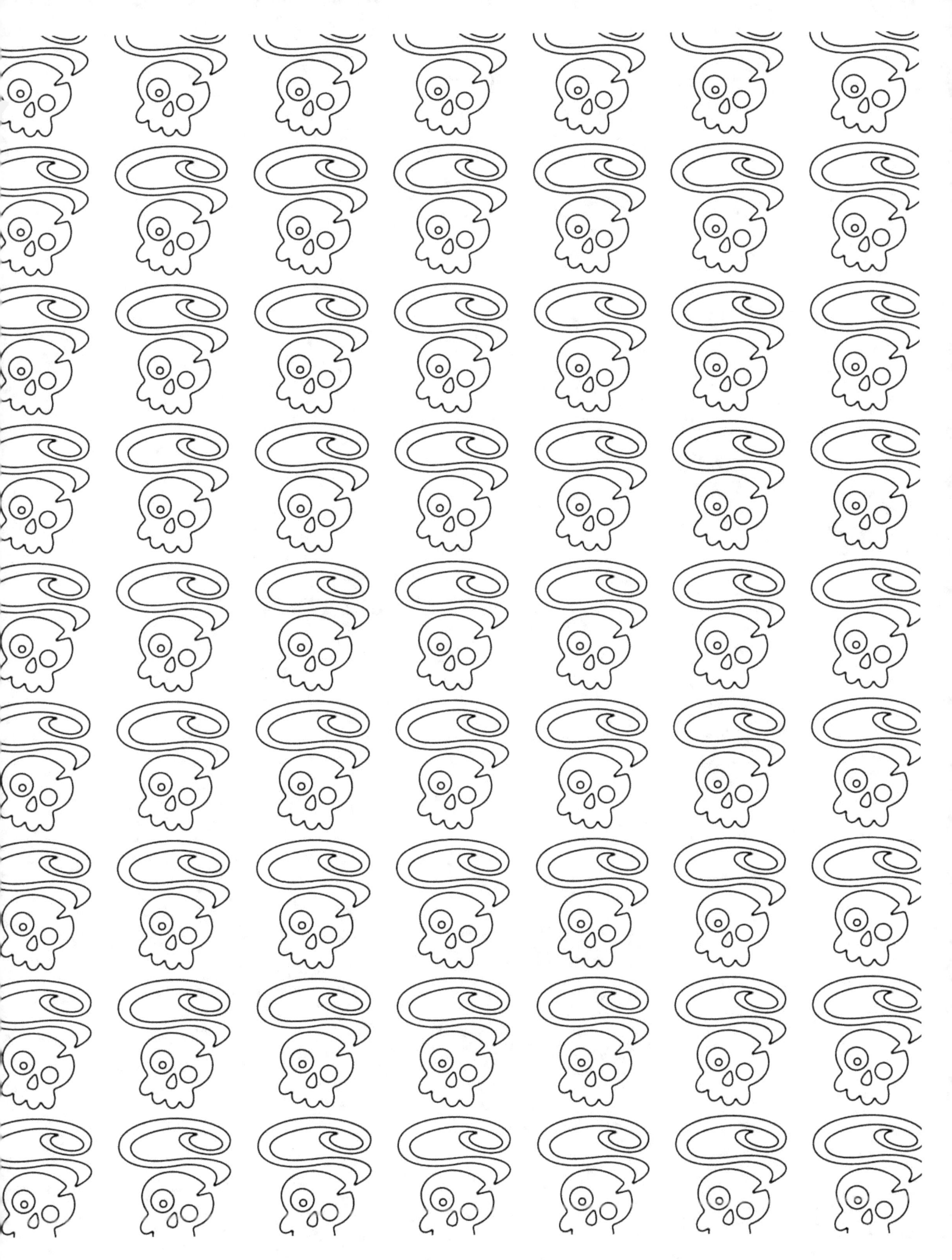

Doodles

Be sure to check out these other titles on Amazon:

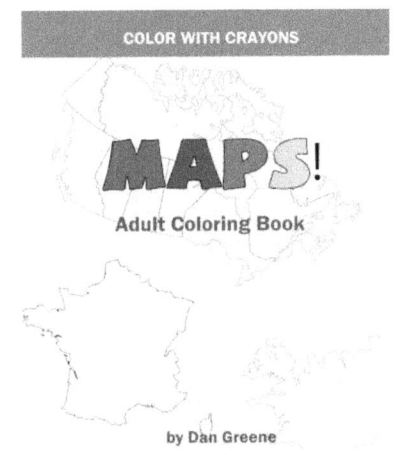

Color With Crayons: Maps!

Color With Crayons: Maps! is a fun coloring book for adults. Are you an adult who wants to color with crayons just like you did when you were a kid? Then this adult coloring book is for you! Color With Crayons: Maps! includes 24 maps for you to color. Lands you can color include: -England and the British Aisles -France -Europe -The United States -Australia -Denmark -Scotland ...and many more!

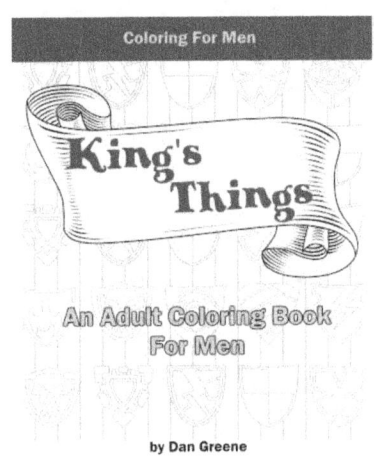

King's Things: An Adult Coloring Book for Men

You won't find hearts or flowers in this coloring book. Instead you'll find things like zombies and viking ships. Relax and color with 17 unique designs made with men in mind. Enjoy coloring in stress-relieving patterns and large geometric shapes. Relax and join in on the fun of adult coloring.

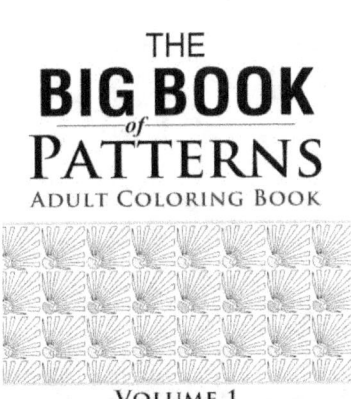

The Big Book of Patterns Volume 1

The Big Book of Patterns Volume 1 is a coloring book for adults or anyone who loves to color! It includes a whopping 50 patterns for hours and hours of coloring fun. Included are mandalas, animal patterns, geometric shapes, stars, hearts, and tons more! Great for coloring with crayons, gel pens, or colored pencils.

www.ingramcontent.com/pod-product-compliance
Lightning Source LLC
Chambersburg PA
CBHW060010210526

45170CB00017B/2143